Salt in the Blood

Salt in the Blood

An autobiography

Ken Pickering

BRAVO ZULU COMMUNICATIONS

To my three 'Js'
who encouraged me to write
and to whom this book is dedicated.

Preface

MEMORY IS THE FACULTY by which things are recalled or kept in the mind. The following are certain memories recorded over a period of sixty years based on my working life experiences.

The described personalities of colleagues are purely as the writer beheld them.

Apologies to those who object to some of the strong shipyard language.

First published in Great Britain in 2008 by 5458 Communications

 Published in 2011 by Bravo Zulu Communications

Text © Ken Pickering
Design and layout © 2011 Bravo Zulu Communications

Designed by Giraffic Design
Edited by Judith Tate and Jill Newton
Reprinted and revised in 2011

ISBN 978-0-9558876-2-8

Contents

1. Introduction

The 4TH FEBRUARY, 1933 was a very special day for Evelyn and Alonzo Pickering, for after having been blessed in the past with three girls Doreen, Muriel and Dorothy they now had a boy whom they named Kenneth Alonzo. Sixteen months later they had another baby girl named Sylvia.

Although my father's one and only Christian name was Alonzo, he was known as Jim by everyone. I believe my mother preferred Jim to Alonzo, so he was stuck with that for the rest of his life. Like all good parents in those days, I was named after my father with the additional name of Kenneth, which was abbreviated to Ken by all except the family.

As a child I would never reveal my second name to anyone for fear of ridicule but as the years passed I became quite proud of having such an unusual name. As far as I know it is of Spanish origin and I was told by a Spanish doctor that one of Spain's champion bullfighters was named 'Alonzo' although I can find no trace or reason why my grandfather and my father should acquire this name. People have suggested to me that it was because they were always 'shooting the bull', but if you believe that, you'll believe anything!

It would appear that being the only boy in the family I would be spoilt - I always contend that my parents were not wealthy enough during the Second World War years to spoil anyone. My father naturally took a keen interest in me, being the only boy. Later in life, my mother showed great affection towards me and yes, she probably did spoil me. Perhaps this was to be expected when all but my eldest sister, Doreen, moved away from the North East.

Prominent in my mind, is the very happy family life we enjoyed together in the early days of the Second World War. I was born in Burton-on-Trent and came to live in Newcastle as a baby. I attended West Walker Primary School, Warrior Street Junior and Senior School and Heaton Technical Senior School. Like many other young students in those days, University was never an option for me, for my parents could not afford the fees, and I had never ever contemplated going in the first place.

Further education for me was three evenings per week at 'Night Classes'.

2. The Naval Yard

I LEFT SCHOOL AT THE AGE OF FIFTEEN and commenced my working life as an office boy at Vickers Naval Yard at Walker-on-Tyne about three miles from the city of Newcastle. This shipyard was always known affectionately as 'The Naval Yard', due to the many naval ships built there.

In order to give one an overall picture of the layout of the shipyard and offices where I worked, a brief description is necessary. The Naval Yard was the largest shipyard of those operating on the River Tyne and had the advantage of being positioned right on the bend of the river, thereby being able to launch its vessels at the river's widest point. This was particularly advantageous when launching large Tankers and Passenger Liners.

Initially the yard had ten building berths, but this was later reduced to seven. These berths varied in size to accommodate the various size ships being built. Apart from having the greatest number of launch ways of all the yards it also possessed the largest standing crane in Europe having a lifting capacity of two hundred and fifty tons. This crane was unique as it had a smaller crane running along its upper structure which handled the lighter loads to be incorporated into the vessels which were being fitted-out alongside the Fitting-Out-Berth.

The Big Crane, as it was affectionately known, was a real asset to the yard as it was able to lift complete engines into the vessels being built, which saved time and money as the only other crane capable of doing this was The Port of Tyne Authority Floating Crane. The floating crane was usually hired by the other yards although if it was already being used then the other yards would hire the Naval Yard's Big Crane. This was expensive because they had the extra cost of having the particular vessel requiring the lift towed up to the Naval Yard.

The workshops and stores within the yard were positioned in accordance with the building and fitting-out of the vessels. These comprised the: Plate Shed, Rolling Mill, Coppersmiths, Plumbers, Blacksmiths, Fitters, Electricians, Joiners and Paint Shops plus the various trade stores and General Store.

At the northern and central part of the yard was the Main Office block which comprised seven floors, communication between which was by two sets of stairs each surrounding a lift, one positioned at the east side and the other the west side of the building.

The ground floor, numbered the first floor, housed the Head Foreman's offices and the Time Office, while the second floor accommodated the Shipyard Managers. The Canteen, Kitchen and Labour Office were positioned on the third floor and the Purchasing Department, Shipping Owners Representatives, Ministry Of Defence, Lloyds and Department of Trade offices were situated on the fourth floor. The fifth floor, generally known as the main floor was occupied by the Directors and their Secretaries, the Staff General Office, the Correspondence Office, the Model Exhibition Hall and the Main Entrance which led out to street level. The sixth and top floor comprised all of the drawing offices, Tracing Office Steel Ordering Office and finally the Printing Room.

3. Office Boy

IT WAS IN THE CORRESPONDENCE OFFICE that I commenced my working life as an office boy on 1 March 1948, a month after my fifteenth birthday. My main job was to deliver internal and external mail throughout the main offices and shipyard workshops. In reality I was a glorified postman. Having said that, I must confess I loved the job for it afforded me the opportunity of meeting and making friends with a vast variety of people from directors to labourers, many to whom I am deeply grateful for their experienced guidance and encouragement to me during my career.

It should be noted that although I had commenced my career at Vickers I had previously applied for a job at C.A. Parsons Electrical Engineering Company. Parsons did not have a vacancy at the time but promised to contact me when one became available, which could take at least eight weeks. Bearing this in mind, I decided in the meantime to get a job elsewhere so that I could help to pay my way at home. How I came to work at Vickers will be revealed later, but back to my job as an office boy.

The head of the Correspondence Office was Ian MacCallum who, as the name implies, was a Scotsman. He lodged with a neighbour of my mother and lived opposite our house at Southfield Terrace in Walker. Our family had known Mr. MacCallum for some time and it was through this friendship that he invited me to start my career in shipbuilding in his department. He was a gentleman in every sense of the word. I am deeply indebted to him for the encouragement and support he gave me in my first year at work, as indeed I am to his deputy, Fred Bolton, for his guidance and support throughout my early years as an apprentice.

The office where I worked was split into three sections, typists on one side, Deputy Manager and Head Clerk's desks in the centre, and the printing machine, office boys' desks and mail sorting table on the other side.

The typing pool of about six young ladies was headed by a very strict and straight-laced spinster, who we office-boys nick-named Miss-Take because when ever anything went wrong it was always someone else's mistake, never hers. The trouble was she was nearly always right.

The typists and office boys were frightened of her for she ran the typing pool with a rod of iron and while she was not directly in charge of us, she would have us running at her beck and call with commands like a sergeant major. It was like being back at school. When she left the room there was always a sigh of relief and it was a signal for the young typists to commence chattering about the previous evening's escapades with their husbands, boyfriends, lovers, etc. The girls always took good care to see that we office boys were not listening, (so they thought), but often we hid behind the printing machine pretending to be working but really enjoying their conversation, particularly the personal tit-bits!

One morning and one afternoon per week I had to attend the company school where we were taught about the different trades within the yard, preparing us for our eventual move into a trade apprenticeship when we reached the age of sixteen. Various subjects were taught throughout the school term, and twice a year we had examinations.

I well remember the mid-term exam paper because the actual paper was sent to our office for printing and my colleague and I had to print the papers. Our boss had not bothered to open the envelope to see what had to be printed, as there was an instruction printed on the envelope requesting fifty copies. You can imagine our surprise at our good fortune, of course it was all right having the questions but we had no answers; however, it was a good start.

The first move my colleague and I made was to contact the rest of the office boys working in the other offices throughout the main building and tell them of our good fortune. Being good business people, we sold each office boy a copy of the exam paper for six old pence. This gave us each a net profit of one shilling and six pence old money, which in those days would enable us to get into the circle of the local cinema, so we were quite happy with our little profit. Come the day of the exams, we all sat there waiting for the paper really feeling good inside knowing full well we were going to do well in these exams. However, we were in for a shock for the exam paper was entirely different to the one we had expected. My colleagues and I were dumbfounded, so much in fact that it took a while for us to get started on the exam paper in front of us.

It was a few weeks later that I found out that the office clerk had checked the copies we had printed before sending them back to the school and wrote a memo to the school telling them that he suspected we had read the exam papers before printing them. So our easy ride through the exams had mis-fired. As it happened I came out top in the exam so it did not make any difference to the outcome, although it taught me a lesson I have never forgotten; honesty is the best policy. Needless to say we had to return our ill-gotten gains.

It was round about this time that my father died at the age of forty-nine. My mother, sisters and I were deeply shocked and I remember feeling at a total loss without him, for he and I were very close. I had virtually worshipped him all of the fifteen years I'd known him. When I was young I followed my father everywhere, in the house or garden, my respect and devotion towards him was immeasurable. I never tired of being in his presence and was always thrilled when he let me share in whatever he was doing. He was patient, kind and generous to his family and neighbours and always ready to teach me how to do practical things from a very early age. I sensed and knew he liked having me around. Yes, he was a sad loss to our family.

A few weeks later a letter arrived from C.A. Parsons inviting me to join them as they now had a vacancy for an apprenticeship in their company. This really put me in a quandary not knowing what to do; whether to go to Parsons, which had been my first choice, or to stay at the Naval Yard where I was making good progress. This was the time I needed my father's advice and he was not there to give it. I felt so helpless and alone, particularly as I did not want to burden my mother with my problems during her bereavement. The decision to stay at the Naval Yard was taken after discussions on my future with Ian MacCallum and Fred Bolton whose advice and guidance at that time were deeply appreciated by me. It would be remiss of me not to mention two other gentlemen who showed kindness and generosity towards my mother and family during our bereavement, namely Captain Sissmore, Personnel Director, and Steve Blackett, Personnel Manager.

In later years, I lived in the same street as Steve Blackett and often travelled to work in his car. This close contact with one another and his keen interest in my career led to a friendship which lasted many years until he finally moved out of the area.

During the period of my work as an office boy one of my duties was to stand in for Sam the lift operator during his lunch break. There were two lifts in the building but only one was normally operated during the day, except on a launch day, when one of my colleagues or I had to help in operating one of them. Sam was a very friendly character who always had a kind word, a smile, and generally a funny story to tell you. He was also the Bookies contact for all horse racing bets which were discreetly placed through Sam. I used to operate the lift during Sam's lunch hour from 1 to 2 pm or sometimes all day if he was off work, sick.

The lifts were the old fashion type with open mesh doors, which enabled you to see the floor you were approaching. Sam taught me all that there was to know about hand operated lifts. His favourite remedy if the lift got stuck between floors was to jump up and down in the lift, the vibration of which supposedly reconnected the well worn electrical contacts which had somehow parted. I could never accept that this was the answer to the problem, however it worked.

Operating a lift up and down seven floors was quite mundane work and in the latter period of the year I operated the lift, the motion quite often made me feel sick. However, not all lift work was boring; there were some lively incidents.

One day while I was on lift duty, I had to pick up the Chairman, Mr Ormston, his Deputy, Mr Houlden, and three or four important Ship Owners in the lift from the Restaurant on the third floor, with the intention of taking them up to the fifth floor. Unfortunately the lift got stuck between the fourth and fifth floor. I must explain that the lift could only be operated manually with a lever moved to the left for up, to the right for down, and to the central position for off. There was also an alarm push button fitted which raised an alarm in the Head Porter's Office at the main entrance where Sam took his packed lunch.

Of all the days, the alarm did not work. When a lift stops between floors your first reaction as operator is to put the operating lever into reverse, in this instance the 'down' position, then in the 'up' position or if that does not work switch off the power for a few seconds then put it back on.

As we were now stuck in the lift between floors, I proceeded to carry out all of the above procedures as instructed by Sam, but to no avail and much to my embarrassment in the presence of my distinguished 'cargo'. There was one other solution and that was to get out through the trap door in the roof of the lift, but with seven people in a lift which takes a maximum of eight, two of which were fairly rotund, this would have been very difficult to say the least.

By this time the Chairman was becoming a little irritable and began to verbally threaten to sack the person who should have been on duty in the Hall Porter's office where the alarm should have sounded, namely Sam. It was at this juncture that I decided, reluctantly, to try Sam's jump remedy in the hope of bridging some electrical contact to make the lift move.

It was unfortunate that I had the operating lever in the down position when I jumped, for the lift suddenly started to descend at a quicker rate than normal, much to the shock of all within who, at the sudden descent, had all left their stomachs somewhere about the fourth floor. After passing two floors I gathered my wits and stopped the lift dead by switching the power off. This action, as you can well imagine, did not go down well with the rest of the party in the lift. Particularly the Chairman who by this time, being one of the more rotund gentlemen in the party, had sunk to his knees with the sudden descent of the lift and was now expressing some very rude words in my direction. This barrage of profane language, much to the amusement of the others present, spurred me into taking further action. I switched the power back on and put the operating handle in the up position, for by now I was desperate to get the lift up to the fifth floor at any cost.

Much to my surprise the lift started to ascend at normal speed up to the required floor where I deposited six bemused gentlemen and one irate Chairman. I smile at the thought of the idiotic things I did to get that lift moving and yet it worked. Mind you I'm sure one or two of my passengers that day were praying when we made that rather speedy descent.

Nothing serious happened with respect to dismissals, all that was done was a complete overhaul of the lift machinery and a new alarm system fitted. Needless to say whenever the Chairman came into the lift while I was operating it, he always made some sarcastic remark like, "We are going to have an easy ride today aren't we son?" No reply was necessary, but my red face conveyed my feelings. Incidentally Sam was quite perturbed at what had happened and said it was unfortunate that I happened to be on duty rather than him, but that was life, everyone has their 'ups and downs'.

My lift experience enabled me to converse with people of various occupations within the company as well as visitors. Strange as it may seem, I think it was my height, which started people off talking to me, for at this time I was 6ft. 4ins. which was exceptionally tall in those days. It was through these brief conversations that I became well known throughout the yard and offices. Being tall does have its advantages although there can be serious disadvantages which I will expand on later.

Halfway through my year as an office boy I decided I would serve an apprenticeship as an electrician. This decision was made initially by the fact that I was making good progress at the yard school where I tended to find more interest in the subject of electrical engineering rather than any of the other trades being taught. Although I must admit I was tempted to take up Joinery as I loved wood - work. I enjoyed the yard school very much. I suppose this was because I was achieving high marks in all my subjects there.

4. Outward Bound

IT WAS AT THIS TIME that the company decided for the very first time to offer to the best under sixteen year old boy and the best apprentice within the company, a month's course at the Outward Bound Sea School at Aberdovey in Wales.

The Outward Bound Sea School was founded in October 1941 by two men of forceful mind and Christian purpose, Laurence Holt and Kurt Hahn, who both loved youth and the sea, and mountains and hills. Laurence Holt knew the sea and seamen; Hahn was famous for his brilliant work as an educationalist at Salem and Gordonstoun. Both had the passion necessary to forge and consolidate their ideas. So contributing to the solution of the problem of how to build citizens able to take full advantage of modern technological knowledge, and yet remain masters of their individual souls and respectful of the individual personalities of their fellow men.

Everything, therefore, at the Outward Bound Sea School is designed to give a boy one more opportunity for self discovery. An apprentice Joiner and I were selected to represent the company on this course. The award to George Downey and me was quite an honour as we were the first representatives from the whole of the North East. Of course there were interviews with the local papers who gave extensive write-ups and photographs of George and me and the story behind our selection.

The course lasted twenty six days and comprised approximately 120 boys of very different social backgrounds to mine, split into ten teams known by the nautical term of 'Watches'. Competition was between 'Watches' rather than individuals, therefore making team work a priority.

Training was intense for the whole of the course. Each boy was set a standard according to his age for sprinting, long distance running, walking, high and long jumping and throwing the javelin, discus and weight. There was also training provided for boat exercises of all kinds under oars, sail and power, as well as a commander course, climbing and long distance walking. Two hours study in the evening on types of sail, flags, sailing techniques, tying knots and Morse code were the order of each day. A very comprehensive course which took place in the month of February.

One unpleasant and chilling experience was having to rise at 6am each morning. We had to don a singlet (tee-shirt), a pair of shorts and sand-shoes (trainers) and run a mile down the road and back before going into open showers in the grounds of the school.

Here each individual 'Watch' member stripped naked and stood under one of a line of cold showers, along with eleven other youths and on a given command we each pulled our individual shower chain which released freezing cold water upon us. This almost took your breath away bearing in mind that this took place in the middle of February with snow covering the ground.

We had to stay under the shower for one minute which was duly timed by our leader. I don't mind admitting that the minute seemed like an eternity. If you released the chain before the minute had elapsed then you had to go back under the shower on your own for another minute under the gaze of all your colleagues and much to their delight at your discomfort. Not an experience I would want to do again I'm sure.

Every four days, each watch took a turn at kitchen duties, which included preparing meals. Each day's activities had to be recorded in a personal log-book. In the final week of the course we were split into groups of five and sent out on a thirty mile expedition across the local mountains and valleys using a very basic in-house printed map. This showed four check-points which had to be visited en-route, although it had a very limited amount of route information. This proved to be quite a strenuous experience, which I recorded in my Log Book.

Just as the highlight of the work on land is the thirty mile expedition, so the most important part of the nautical training is the three day cruise on board the 'Garibaldi', a sixty ton sailing Ketch. Cruising for four days in the Irish Sea proved to be very uncomfortable owing to the very rough sea, part of a force seven gale. Apart from being sea-sick, I learnt how to sail by compass, rig sails, scrub decks and cook meals, which is a nightmare when you are feeling sea-sick. The only enjoyable and interesting part of the voyage was steering the ship by compass at night under the stars, which is when I really felt I was a sailor!

I think all of us at the end of the trip were glad to get ashore, although when we did, we found it hard to walk straight after the continuous rolling and pitching of the ship.

The course itself was a great success as far as I was concerned for it seemed to bring out qualities of leadership, physical stamina and endurance which I never realised I possessed. I learnt a great deal about myself and indeed other people from different walks of life on the course and I firmly believe that it laid the foundation of my character and attitude to other people for the duration of my working life.

The only disappointment was that I put an extra half-inch on to my height according to the school medical staff. This now made me six foot four and a half inches in height, to which I have remained right up to the present day.

At that time I was very slim built and really outgrowing my strength even though I enjoyed good healthy meals, which my mother seemed to provide out of nothing during those latter days of food rationing.

I found it hard on my return to work to get into the mundane sequence of sorting and delivering mail etc after such an exciting and stimulating adventure, which it all seemed to me, for I had never been any further from Newcastle than West Hartlepool where I spent occasional summer holidays with my aunts and uncles, on my mother's side of the family. After a few days I was back into the swing of things doing my daily tasks and in-between times relating my experiences at the school to my colleagues.

5. More Office Escapades

Every year at the yard apprentice school there was a spring-clean of the classrooms organised by the lecturers and carried out by the pupils. I recall that the classrooms had very high ceilings, up to about twenty feet in height and it was my task along with a fellow pupil to wash the top of these walls. I assumed they picked me because of my height for reaching, but in any case I still needed a ladder.

I drew the short straw for who had to go up the ladder. Up I went with my bucket and cloth and commenced washing the wall whilst my colleague held the bottom of the ladder. After a while my helper left for some reason without telling me. Bearing in mind there was probably more water on the floor than in the bucket, the top of the ladder started to slide down the wall, with me precariously hanging on with one hand and trying to steady the bucket with the other. It didn't take long for the ladder and me to reach the bottom where I somehow finished up with my head in the bucket amidst loud cheering and laughter from my colleagues. Fortunately there were no broken bones, just a few bruises on my head and arms which took most of the weight when I landed. My colleagues informed me that it would have made a good comedy film but I was not amused. One good thing that came out of it was that there was no more spring cleaning by the pupils, the staff realising how dangerous it could be.

One afternoon while printing some urgent documents during the lunch hour, I ran out of paper so I had to go to the stock-room for replenishments. As I unlocked and opened the door to go in, who should be standing very close together at the far end of the room but my boss and his secretary.

I thought nothing of it at the time, got the paper I wanted and left. It wasn't until I got back to the office and thought about it, that I realised something must be going on between them when they were together in a locked room. There was nothing wrong with that as far as I was concerned, he was a bachelor and she a spinster and it was their lunch break after all. It wasn't until some weeks later when returning to the office after normal working hours to retrieve some keys I had left behind that I saw them embracing through the interconnecting glass door between his office and the Correspondence Office. I then realised there was some sort of love affair between them. Fortunately they didn't see me, and I was pleased they hadn't for I would not have wanted to embarrass them, particularly my boss, who I held in high esteem.

My visits down the Yard delivering mail gave me an opportunity to see this great shipyard in production. The various sights and sounds from which one could recognise and determine the tasks being performed were truly amazing. Also the tremendous size of steel plates being assembled on the launch ways; the shifting of cranes with swaying loads and the movement of men, like ants, each busy with their allotted task, never ceased to fascinate me. Passing through the yard into the various workshops, I was intrigued by all the machines and equipment which went into the building of ships.

As I had to deliver mail to the Head Foreman's Office within the various workshops, this meant I became very friendly with some of the workmen and their Foreman. This friendship was particularly appreciated during the winter months when my hands would be numb with the cold. There would always be the offer of a mug of tea to warm me up and a real Geordie chat about Newcastle United or the job, preferably in that order of importance.

Of all the mail deliveries I had to make there was one I was very reluctant to carry out and that was to the Tracing Office, which was occupied by some ten to fifteen females, most of them in their teens.

The office was supervised by two middle aged spinsters, one of whom was named Joyce, the head tracer, who became a very good friend of mine later in my career. I really did dread going into this office for the door entrance was at the opposite end to the supervisor's office and the thirty yards walk down the office always seemed like a mile to me. This was because as soon as any male entered the office every female head would look-up from their tracing board and stare at him, giggle and pass amusing remarks amongst themselves about the poor embarrassed male intruder. In my case, I felt like a solitary fly on a web where dozens of spiders were waiting to pounce on their prey. It was really embarrassing, for at that time I was a shy and quiet type of person, not particularly interested in girls; football and tennis were my main interests. Mind you some of the lads used to lap up the female attention.

6. The Apprentice

AFTER A YEAR, at the age of sixteen, it was time for me to begin my apprenticeship in the shipyard.

In one respect it was sad that I was leaving a lot of good friends in the office, some of whom I will never forget, for their kindness shown to me during difficult times. Yet here I was moving out into the real world of shipbuilding, 'down the yard' as the workmen would say. Although I found it exciting, I also felt a little trepidation at the thought of moving into this vast noisy mechanised set-up. However this was to be the start of my career and I chose the electrical field as a trade to make my mark in life.

My first day was one of total apprehension for everything was new to me, although I must admit I knew my way around having passed through every department delivering mail.

One of the main differences in working in the yard as against the offices was that I now had to commence work at 7.30am rather than 8.45am. This did not bother me unduly as I had always found it easy to rise early when required. One advantage was that I only lived ten minutes walk from the yard which meant I could get home for dinner each day. I should mention that all the family had dinner at midday with the exception of my father who had his about 6pm.

Having started to work in the yard, I now had to use the yard entrance, which was another couple of hundred yards east of the office entrance. It was quite a long walk down to the 'check-out' office where I used to check-in every morning and afternoon.

The yard must have been about sixty feet below street level and three foot above the river at high tide. The long sloping walk from the entrance to the yard had a railway line running parallel with it with a grass bank on one side and a fence on the other side through which you could look down upon the various workshops and river jetty. Walking into the electricians' shop that first morning was like starting school; I was nervous and very apprehensive. However, the men were friendly and made me welcome, even though they consistently made detrimental remarks about my height.

There were about fifteen men working in the electricians' shop, the majority of who were electricians. The rest consisted of clip-makers (men who shaped aluminium, galvanised steel and brass clips to hold the cables being installed on board the ships), two plumbers who looked after all pipework and finally a joiner who provided all the woodwork items required by the electricians. There were also three or four electricians assigned to maintain the shipyard plant machinery.

In the centre of the workshop stood a gas heated metal trough which contained molten solder which was used for the repair of motor windings and the connection of cable terminals etc. This was the warmest spot in the workshop so everyone used to congregate here before commencing work, particularly on the cold winter mornings. It was also the place where one could hear all the local gossip about what was happening on the ships or the escapades of the previous night's social events!

Next to the main entrance to the shop was a set of stairs leading to the Foreman's and Head Foreman's Offices which were built on stilts and from where an overall view of the workshop could be seen. At the opposite end was the Shop Foreman's Office which housed a foreman called Tommy Coxon, a very strict disciplinarian who, all the time I knew him, never smiled, however he was a good electrician.

Some of the journeymen (workmen who are qualified tradesmen) sat on stools at their workbenches where they assembled various pieces of electrical equipment. I was assigned to assist one of these electricians and hopefully learn something about the trade. One day I felt the wrath of Tommy Coxon, much to my surprise, as I thought I had done nothing wrong, as I sat down on a nearby stool to rest my legs. Unknowingly I had committed the unpardonable offence to which all apprentices succumb in their first year of training, which is to sit down on the job.

I had been sitting on the stool for less than half a minute when Tommy's voice screamed out at me from his office, "Get off your arse boy, where do you think you are, Butlins Holiday Camp?" I immediately half jumped, half fell off that stool, much to the delight of my fellow workmates. Tommy then strode down to where I was and proceeded to give me a lecture on the acceptable and unacceptable procedures that one was allowed to exercise within his domain.

I had learnt lesson number one, although I felt the telling off was unjustified because at that time I was physically outgrowing my strength and could not stand in the one position for very long without beginning to feel faint. These fainting bouts first took place when I was at Heaton Technical School during the morning assemblies. I used to get through the first hymn all right then in the middle of the prayer I would flake out. It was a long way to fall but fortunately no damage was done during the many times I fainted. It became such a habit that the Headmaster excused me from attending assemblies. Having said that, Tommy Coxon was not to know that and Tommy's rule was that no apprentice was allowed to sit down on the job, fainting or no fainting!

Not long after this incident one of the electricians sent me up to the Head Foreman's office for a 'long stand', he explained to me that it was an object for measuring time. I dutifully went up the stairs to his office, knocked on the door, went in and requested the 'long stand'.

The Head Foreman said he was quite busy but if I waited outside his office door he would see that I got the 'long stand'. I must have stood there for about half an hour and nothing happened so I thought I had better remind him that I was still waiting for this long stand. On entering his office he turned towards me and asked "How long have you been standing outside my office?" I said "About half an hour", to which he replied, smiling, "Well that seems to be a long enough stand for you", whereupon I bid a hasty retreat feeling very much the idiot! You can imagine the ribbing I had to endure from my colleagues when I returned to my workbench.

In the electricians' workshop there was a caged area where the joiner, Bertie Wolf, 'hung out.' I use that expression because he never seemed to do any joinery work there. His main task was seeing that the electricians working on the ships were supplied with any wooden items that they required, such as switch blocks, light fitting bases, etc. These items were manufactured in the main joiners' shop at the east end of the yard, but supplied to Bertie for distribution to the electricians. The only bit of joinery Bertie had to do was modifications where necessary. The nice thing about Bertie was that he would do anything for anybody. Nothing was a trouble to him, although you had to be very patient at times, for everything got done at his pace which was not always too quick, though whatever he did was done well. I got to know Bertie well over the years and found him to be a genuine character who always had a tale or two to tell. I found out later that he lived in the St. Anthony's area about half a mile from me and was part of the Wolf family, who were prominent members of the local Methodist Church there.

The two plumbers assigned to work in the electricians' shop were, in my eyes, two old men; one was tall and skinny, the other was short and tubby and both were very much alike in their ways. They were also gentlemen in every sense of the word, neither showing any signs of anger, distress or irritation when the job wasn't going smoothly. The taller of the two was very friendly and taught me a lot about plumbing, although I was always a little embarrassed when talking to him for my eyes were always attracted to his nose which dripped continuously throughout the day. I never ever saw him use a handkerchief, only the sleeve of his boiler suit which by the end of the week had quite a polish on it; I used to wonder if his wife knew what the shine was!

I once asked him why he never used a handkerchief, he said "it runs that much it wouldn't be worth the effort, anyway it helps to oil the pipe bending machine I work on". Enough said, I think. He also always had a pipe stuck in his mouth upside down, which was only lit up at break times, and then you couldn't see him for smoke. He really was a loveable character who had a smile that exposed several missing front teeth and those that remained were stained a deep brown colour from his pipe smoking.

After about three months I was beginning to be accepted as part of the shop team although I still had to put up with a lot of skit about my height. I remember one day when the foreman was out of the shop I went over to talk to one of the clip-makers whose job was to make all the various shaped clips for the cable runs on the ships. This was a noisy part of the shop because of the constant hammering by the clip-makers as they shaped the clips.

I parked myself on the bench and was conversing as best I could over the noise when the foreman returned. I immediately jumped down from the bench only to feel and hear a tearing of cloth. Yes, it was my boiler suit, which now had a large tear in the backside and the torn piece of material left nailed to the bench. As you can guess, while I had been talking, one of the other clip-makers had nailed part of my boiler suit to the bench. I naturally, hadn't heard him with all the banging going on. Needless to say my mother wasn't very pleased about it when I got home. Lesson number two: don't sit on the workbench.

In the workshop at one end, there was a section for the use of the plant electricians who maintained all the electrical equipment throughout the yard. The shop had a cat they called "Sparky' (a big ginger tom) who at night used to go rat hunting round the shop which was infested with them. 'Sparky' would catch quite a few rats and play with them before devouring them.

Some of the plant electricians, who were on standby in the shop were not content to just watch 'Sparky' at play, they would get one of the rats (still alive and kicking) pin it down on the bench with a leather strap across its back so that it couldn't escape. They would then proceeded to wire one back leg to a positive terminal and the front leg to a negative terminal of the electricity supply through a rheostat which allowed the operator to regulate the amount of electricity flowing when the power was switched on.

It was worse than a horror film. As the power was allowed to flow through the rat, it would then start to twitch and kick and the more the current was increased the more the rat jumped, squirmed and squealed, until finally an increase in current would kill it, much to the sadistic delight of those watching.

I do not like rats but I detested this barbaric cruelty, fortunately this so-called game was stopped by the night shift foreman who caught them, when he had heard the screams of one of the rats whilst he was in his office.

A party of Japanese businessmen came to visit the Naval Yard. When they returned to Japan they were summoned before the Emperor who asked for their impressions of Geordieland. Your illustrious Highness, said one Japanese, I was amazed that the natives of Tyneside speak fluent Japanese. I was inspecting one of the ships in the yard when I distinctly heard one workman say to another, "Himate Hoya Hammer ower heya!" For those who cannot read Japanese "Excuse me friend would you pass me the hammer over here".

There are lots of queer and funny goings-on inside a shipyard.

7. My First Ship

Aꜰᴛᴇʀ ꜱᴇʀᴠɪɴɢ ᴛʜᴇ ꜰɪʀꜱᴛ ꜱɪx ᴍᴏɴᴛʜꜱ of my apprenticeship in the workshop I was assigned to work on my first ship under a foreman called Jack Bell. Now in those days (I say that because it's different now) you had a foreman, marker-offs (they marked out the job, prepared the cable routes and requisitioned all the electrical material required for the installation of the vessel concerned) the journeymen (time-served electricians) and the apprentices.

There were generally two foremen and three marker-offs per vessel, depending on the size of the ship being built. Jack Bell was one of a number of foremen assigned to a ship called S.S. Strathmore (S.S. meaning Steam Ship). This was a 23,000 ton liner which had arrived at the yard to be converted from her war time duties as a troop ship plying soldiers to the Middle East back to a luxury liner for the transport of passengers to the Middle East and Australia.

The ship was a huge vessel twelve decks high and over 100 yards (90 metres) long and fitted with Parsons Marine turbines for propulsion and one large funnel to exhaust the unwanted gases. She was capable of a maximum speed of twenty knots and a cruising speed of eighteen knots. The Ministry of Defence had finished with her services and had handed her back to her owners P.&O. (Peninsular and Oriental Steam Navigation Company), who were now having her converted back to a passenger liner.

By the time I was assigned to work on this vessel, she had been completely stripped out leaving only the outer shell and inboard steel bulkheads standing. Just for the benefit of the uninitiated, on a ship, the bulkhead is the wall, the deck is the floor and the deckhead is the ceiling.

Well, here I was on my first ship on a cold February morning waiting for my first task as an apprentice electrician with mixed feelings; excited and yet nervous about what lay ahead for me. After waiting around at the gangway entrance for some considerable time a very small man dressed in a navy blue boiler suit and a dirty looking cap came up to me introduced himself as Bobby Holland and led me away down into the bowels of the ship. He took me into a huge working space, which I afterwards discovered was the Galley. Within this space was a small electrical switchboard room where the men working under Bobby kept their coats, bags, etc. and where they congregated for their tea breaks.

By this time it was 9.00am, time for the men's tea break, so most of Bobby's squad of men were coming into the room for their break by the time I arrived. "Hello who's the big fellow? Is it cold up there son? Is there any snow on top of ya heed?" These were just a few of the teasing greetings I had to endure that first morning, however it was all said in good fun, although as I said before, being a little shy, I was embarrassed by it all.

The biggest laugh for the men was that I was standing there, all six foot four and a half of me, alongside Bobby who was only five feet tall; it was a case of the long and the short of it. Funny enough, there were quite a few tall men in the squad and it was Bobby's boast that he had the biggest squad on the ship! He was a good tradesman always willing to help anyone in difficulties and readily prepared to teach anyone the tricks of the trade. As a Marker-off, Bobby would take me with him to check whether the cabins centre lights were positioned correctly. I if I could walk under the fitting without hitting my head then it was positioned correctly, if not then it had to be moved. I suppose you could say I was Bobby's 'yard stick'!

In those days there were no safety helmets, you wore a cap or a beret. I preferred a beret, but it didn't save my head from receiving some nasty blows in some of the more confined spaces within the ship. I suppose that's why I haven't got much hair on top now, it's all been scraped off by the top door frame of the many doorways I've passed through!

Being a new apprentice on board I was ripe for the pranks of my fellow workmates. One day the whole squad of electricians and I as the apprentice were all lined up along one of the decks pulling a large cable in and feeding it through the various bulkheads it had to pass. During a break in the task, one of the men turned to me and asked me what height I was. I replied giving him my exact height. He said "I don't believe you, lets measure you; stand up against that steel bulkhead and I will mark your height in chalk". Well, I did as I was told not suspecting any pranks as they only wanted to measure me. They placed me so that I was standing perfectly erect with the heels of my boots and my head touching the steel bulkhead. So far so good, as I thought, but just as I thought they were going to mark my height there was this almighty thud on the steel bulkhead I was leaning against. I thought my head was going to explode with the vibration of force reverberating through the whole of my body from the blow struck on the other side of that bulkhead. Unknown to me there had been somebody on the other side of the bulkhead ready to hit it with a ten pound sledge-hammer when given the signal. My body tingled all that day and as you can imagine, I had a rather nasty headache afterwards to say the least. My work colleagues thought it a huge joke and told me they had measured seven foot four when the hammer hit the bulkhead! Another experience learning to be an electrician.

One of the first tasks an apprentice is given when he is allotted to work with a journeyman electrician is to make the tea for him at nine o' clock in the morning and at three o' clock in the afternoon. I must emphasise that at this time there were no official tea breaks allowed, so tea drinking had to be done discreetly out of sight of the foremen and managers. Bearing this in mind, the making and drinking of tea became a battle of wits between the participants and the managerial staff. Each workman had his own enamelled metal can in which the water for the tea would be boiled. He would also bring with him each day two brews of tea, one for the morning and one for the afternoon with sugar and milk according to his taste.

Now there were three methods of boiling the can. First, find a Riveter's brazier and hold the can above it with a pair of metal tongs, till the water boiled. Second, heat it with a blow–lamp. Third, insert a spiral element wire connected to the main electricity supply into the water in the can. The third method of heating the metal can was only used by the electricians as it could be dangerous, as I found out on numerous occasions. If you did not get the element perfectly centred over the can, then the element would sometimes touch the side of the metal can giving you a nasty shock.

The most popular method was the Riveter's brazier, if there was one on board. I say this because at this time 'all welded' ships were beginning to be built and riveted ships were being phased out. However during my first year on the ships I was assigned to one which had Riveters on board.

On one occasion I had two cans of water to boil, one for my mate and one for the marker-off, so I set off looking for a Riveter's brazier which I duly found and got permission from him to boil my two cans. I should mention at this point that the can was boiled with the loose tea in the bottom of it and sometimes with a spoonful or two of condensed milk as this saved on fresh milk and sugar. This was how I learnt to drink shipyard tea in its many forms, with or without milk, with milk and sugar, without milk but with sugar, with fresh milk or with condensed milk. I never knew what type of brew I would be drinking from one day to the next but it seemed to be refreshing at the time.

Anyway back to the brazier; as I had two cans and there was only one pair of tongs available I had to stand one can on top of the coke fire while I held the other over the fire with the tongs. So far so good; the water was just coming to the boil when someone shouted "here comes the manager!" Well, I've never attempted to move so fast in my life. I say attempted because things didn't go as planned. I immediately removed the can I held in the tongs and put it down on the deck, then picked up the other can by the handle forgetting that by this time it was boiling hot. I dropped the can, the contents of which went all over the fire and doused it, much to the annoyance of the brazier attendant who then started to give me a right mouthful of shipyard language, not to be

34

repeated here. I then stepped back only to knock over the other can. I got out my handkerchief, grabbed the cans and sped off back to my work station before the manager caught me. Actually it may have been better to have been caught by the manager than suffer the abuse I had to endure from my work colleagues. There was no tea that morning, only moans about my inability to provide the nine o' clock cuppa.

Lesson number three: always save the tea no matter what.

Once a week, the shipyard manager met with the ship's manager, the trade managers and foremen with the purpose of inspecting the ship to view the progress of outfitting trades and to ascertain that the work completed was in accordance with the scheduled programme. This team was easily distinguishable by the fact that the managers wore bowler hats and the foremen trilby hats.

This inspection always kept everyone on their toes, all tradesmen and apprentices would be working at their allotted work stations. Certainly, no tea drinking or skiving when the shipyard manager and his team were on board. The ship's jungle telegraph generally warned us that the team were on board or approaching our vicinity. This didn't always work for the shipyard manager used to change the day of his inspection and if the jungle telegraph failed then you could be certain someone would be caught drinking tea, reading a newspaper or skiving. The culprit was usually given a reprimand or, depending on what mood the shipyard manager was in, he could be sacked. Unfortunately the shipyard manager at the time was a man called Brown, better known in the yard as 'Sackum' (sack-him) Brown. He was a mean, arrogant and miserable man who hadn't a pleasant or kind word for anybody. He was generally feared throughout the yard by all personnel mainly because he would think nothing of sacking a person for the most trivial of matters. It was a happy day in the yard when he retired.

Having said that his successor, Henry Snaddon, a Scotsman, only known as 'Snaddon' wasn't much better. He was a very stout man with bright coloured cheeks, which suggested that he had high blood pressure probably due to all the weight he had to carry. He was another manager who had no qualms about sacking anyone.

My first unintentional acquaintance with him was when he came aboard the ship on his own and was walking down one of the passageways where I happened to be working. I was standing on a stool clipping some cables up on the deckhead and as there was very little room to get passed he had to try and squeeze past me. I was unaware of his presence, being engrossed in what I was doing, so when he tried to pass, he pushed me off the stool whereupon I fell on top of his head pushing his bowler hat down over his eyes. When I picked myself up from the deck, there was 'Snaddon' struggling to get his bowler hat over his eyes back into its normal position. How I didn't burst out laughing I'll never know. I think I was too terrified as to what he was going to say or do with me. When he eventually got the bowler up over his eyes, he looked at me and said in his broad Scottish twang, "What are you staring at laddie? Get on with your bloody job", and then stomped off down the passage much to my surprise. Whenever he saw me after that incident, he just used to nod. I'm sure he remembered that I was the same lad who delivered his mail the previous year. Throughout the yard 'Snaddon' like his predecessor, was not liked by the men. It was a pity that he had this nasty streak in him for he was a good shipbuilder.

I enjoyed my work experience on the 'Strathmore'; little did I know at the time that this ship was to play an important role in my career at a later date.

8. 'Bomber'

My NEXT ASSIGNMENT was to a Blue-Funnel (Alfred Holt Line) ship, which was still on the launch-way. This was quite an experience for me because there was just the steel shell and a few decks of the ship erected at the time she was due to be launched in about a month. There was however, machinery fitted in the engine room which allowed the electrician's 'marker-off' to prepare his cable runs.

It was the engine room that was to be my work place for the next three months or more under the supervision of a marker-off called Jimmy Topping. Jimmy and I were the only electricians on board, the rest of the men were either platers, riveters, welders or labourers.

It was strange working in those conditions, all this bare steel around with very little machinery installed; it was a very cold environment to work in. It wasn't long before the ship reached the stage where Jimmy could utilise a few electricians on the job. So when he was allotted about four men to work in the engine room he assigned me to assist one of them with a view to increasing my knowledge of the electrical trade.

The electrician I was assigned to assist was a broad Geordie called 'Bomber' Adams. 'Bomber' was a nick-name derived from his days of flying in bomber aircraft during the war for the Royal Canadian Air Force. No one ever knew 'Bomber's' real Christian name. 'Bomber' was a real Geordie character who stood no nonsense from anyone, said what he thought and expressed himself quite often in strong language. He was the type who grew on you once you got to know him. If you were on the receiving end of his swearing, well, his bark was worse than his bite, you just accepted it as his normal way of conversation.

It was my first taste of real shipyard language and it's funny that after a while, no matter how hard you tried not to, you would find yourself using the same strong language, particularly when the job wasn't going right or if you were in the company of men who were regularly swearing. Outside the yard I found no difficulty in refraining from swearing, I suppose that's because it was never used at home.

One marker-off (another Jimmy) I worked with used every other word as a swear word. After a few weeks I got fed up with his continual swearing and told him so. He said he couldn't help it, so I suggested we have a swear box so whoever swore had to put a penny (old money) in the box. The scheme only lasted two days as Jimmy had contributed nearly a pound in those two days, which was an awful lot of swearing (there were 240 pennies to the pound). Fortunately for me I only worked with Jimmy for three weeks. For all of Jimmy's swearing, he was a good mate, kind hearted and always prepared to help anyone in difficulties.

'Bomber' was nowhere near as bad as Jimmy with his language. He was a very forceful character who always commandeered the conversation either one to one or in a group, but I suppose that was because he was intelligent, knew his trade well and had travelled quite a bit. I learnt a lot about the electrical trade from 'Bomber' and I enjoyed working with him. I found him to be very protective in the sense that he wouldn't let anybody pick on me. I was his apprentice and as far as he was concerned, I was going to be the best!

Working in the engine room there were some extremely physical jobs to be carried out but that was no problem to Bomber for he was quite strong. He obviously kept himself in good shape by exercising. It was during the periods of working with him that he would recall his wartime experiences. He had been a 'bomb-aimer' in the Royal Canadian Air Force during the war. He had me spellbound with some of the tales he had to relate, some amusing, some more serious, but all fascinating to hear.

During my apprenticeship with Bomber there used to be regular weekly power cuts, mainly during the winter months, when all the lights would go out for anywhere between ten minutes and up to an hour. When this occurred, Bomber would get a couple of candles out of his toolbox, light them, give one to me and off we'd go down to the Shaft Tunnel. This was a long steel tunnel which ran from the engine room to the aft end of the ship and housed the shaft which turned the propeller. This space was always quiet and out of the way of most workmen and managers. Once Bomber and I got to the shaft tunnel we would place the candles on top the shaft then wait for three or four colleagues to turn up before commencing to play cards. We all stood round the candles playing a game called 'Chase the Ace' for a half-penny a game which could last about two or three minutes depending on the cards. No great fortune was ever made, hence no great loss either. These games would go on until the lights came back on and sometimes even longer, so engrossed would the card players be in 'Chasing the Ace'. Many is the time the marker-off would have to come down to the tunnel to see where we were and get us back to our work station.

I used to look forward to this little card school. Not because we won much but we had some good laughs, particularly when a draught would blow the candles out. Then Bomber would express his feelings by voicing the choicest Shipyard language you could wish to hear, much to the amusement of the rest of us.

When you worked in the Engine room in the early 'fitting out' stages, there was very little machinery of any kind fitted, hence there would be a huge void between the engine room floor level up to the entrance into the engine room. From the entrance down to the engine room floor level there would be a wooden ladder anywhere up to about forty feet long to allow access. I dreaded having to climb up or down this ladder because I've always been nervous of heights. Not only that, if there was more than one person on the ladder at a time and you were not in 'step-phase' with them, then the ladder would sway back and forwards each step you took, which was quite a frightening experience. Of course if you were on the ladder when 'Bomber' was on, it became even more frightening, for he would purposely make the ladder sway by rocking back and forward when he reached the middle of it. I need not relate the abusive language shouted at 'Bomber'.

Sadly my period of apprenticeship with 'Bomber' came to an end when he was sent to work on another vessel. I'll always remember him, not only for his instruction in the advancement of my apprenticeship, but also for his valuable patience, understanding and friendship towards me.

9. No Crossing Your Legs

I T'S A WONDERFUL EXPERIENCE working on ships. The only snag is during the building of them there are no toilet facilities on board. If you felt the urge to go empty your tank, as the men would say, then you went ashore. There were a few toilets scattered around the yard but the main toilet was positioned centrally between the launch-ways and the fitting out berths. Depending where the ship you were working on was positioned, it could be quite a long walk to the main toilet. If you only wanted a 'run-off' then you would go to the toilet local to the ship. However this proved to be too much of a burden to some men who used to go out on the open deck and 'pee' over the side into the river. This was OK, if there was no one around at the time or if there were just men in the vicinity but we used to have women cleaners on board and if they suddenly made an appearance then it became embarrassing because once you had started it was difficult to stop! Some of the women's comments had to be heard to be believed. I, like the rest of the men, used the 'over the rail' method a few times, mainly because it was the quickest way to relieve yourself, until I was caught by one of the women. She called me over and spelt out in no uncertain terms that she was surprised that I could do such a thing. She had recognised me from my work station which she swept daily and sometimes chatted to me. I was so embarrassed. Never again, did I use the ship's side method of relief.

One day my mate and I happened to be working out on the open deck when two workmen came along sheepishly looking to see if there was any one around. Seeing only us they started to 'pee' over the side in unison. Suddenly

I heard shouting from over the side of the ship. On looking over there was a small open boat tied alongside with two men in and they were shouting their heads off as the two up on deck had 'peed' all over them. You couldn't help but see the funny side of it. As for the two men on deck, they scampered off as quickly as they could without any apology.

My mate, in typical Yard fashion, declared that the lesson there was always look over the side before you 'pee' and make sure you know which way the wind is blowing. While on the subject of toilets, I must tell you about the main toilets because they were unique. You've never seen anything like them. They consisted of about twelve cubicles all in a line but instead of a toilet basin there was an open metal trough with a wooden seat fitted on top of the trough. This trough ran through the cubicles from one end to the other and was higher at number one cubicle than at number twelve cubicle. Each cubicle had its own water flushing system which ran into the trough beneath the seat. Hence, if you were in number say, six cubicle and there was someone in number one, then if they flushed the toilet before you had left, then their waste flowed down-hill in the trough underneath you. As you can see, it paid to get a low numbered cubicle.

I was assured by the person who told me and it was later confirmed by others that the following was perfectly true: one Monday morning, as usual every cubicle was occupied, for most of the men would have been out on the beer over the weekend. Well, one joker had gone into number one cubicle, put a match to an oily rag, flushed the toilet then dropped the flaming rag into the water whereupon it floated down the trough still alight, much to the discomfort of those in the other cubicles who got singed as the rag passed beneath them. More bad language. That was the last of the 'phantom toilet igniter,' for after complaints to the management, new up- to-date toilets were fitted.

10. Not Perquisite

As an apprentice it was my job to provide the tradesman I was working with and my 'marker off' with firewood to take home each night. We were still in the era of coal fires those days. Just about every yard worker had a wartime khaki haversack about 9 inches wide by 12 inches long by 4 inches deep, which was a convenient size as two lengths of timber cut to the right dimensions would fit in just nicely. The main use of the haversack was, of course, to carry a man's bait (refreshments).

The outside decks of most ships were covered in teak planking and this was the perfect wood for the fire as it was slow burning and gave off a lot of heat. Each night about half an hour before finishing time, I would go looking for lengths of this decking to cut up into pieces suitable to fit my workmates' haversacks. Sometimes if there weren't any cut lengths I would have to cut up a new plank which was always a risk because it would have been instant dismissal if caught.

One evening just before finishing time, word went round that the gate-men were inspecting every haversack as the men left the yard. It was quite a long walk from the yard up to the gate along a road which had railings on one side and looked down onto the workshops and a railway line bank side on the other When I eventually left the yard and commenced walking up the exit road I was amazed to see the whole of the bank side covered in pieces of wood, cable, pipe, etc. These great piles of material, laid out along a 100 yard stretch of the bank side, were the ill–gotten gains of the workmen who had disposed of them before reaching the entrance gate where the inspection was taking place. They reckon it took three lorry loads to shift all of the materials dumped that night.

The management were not very pleased to hear about the amount of materials that were intended to be stolen, hence random inspections by the gate-men were the order of the day. However, the inspections did not stop the men taking wood out of the yard. They just adopted a different method of removal. Suddenly quite a few of the men on their way out of the yard developed a limp. This was due to them having a length of wood stuck down one leg of their trousers. There was no end to the different methods of taking material out of the yard.

One snowy winter evening, while walking up towards the gate at finishing time, I noticed to my left that there were two men pulling a rope on the end of which was a sledge. A man standing on the sledge was marking time as it was pulled along. This was so that there would be no gap in the crowd for the gate-men to notice anything suspicious and the marking time would look from the gatehouse as though the guy on the sledge was just walking out of the yard. This happened quite a few times when it snowed during the run up to Christmas.

There was also a period when one worker went out of the yard pushing a wheelbarrow, which the gate-man ignored seeing as the barrow was empty. This same workman continued to push an empty wheelbarrow out of the yard each night for the whole of that week until it was discovered that he was steeling wheelbarrows from the yard and selling them.

One of the worst cases of theft happened to a work mate, an electrician, who wanted to take a small tin of carbon tetrachloride out of the yard without being caught. Carbon tetrachloride is a very strong cleaning agent for electrical equipment which has to be handled with care for it stings and burns if it comes in contact with a person's skin. He duly filled a used tin he had found with this tetrachloride, put the lid on and tucked it down inside his underpants ready to leave the yard when the finishing - time siren blew. When the siren blew he duly set off up the bank amidst the other ten thousand and more workmen confident that he would not be caught. I can't remember how it happened but when he was about fifty yards from the gate, the lid of the tin had worked loose and the carbon tetrachloride liquid spilt out over his private parts and ran down his legs which consequently burnt his skin. I believe he ran home in agony once he got through the gate. It was about a fortnight before he returned to work, so it proved to be a costly piece of theft.

There was another workman who thought he'd take about twenty yards of lead covered cable out of the yard. Now how on earth do you walk out with twenty yards of lead covered cable without been seen? Simple, you wrap it round your waist underneath your shirt so that it just looks like you've put on a bit of weight. A perfect way of getting the cable out without being caught, we all thought, except the workman who attempted it wrapped the cable round his middle too tight and unfortunately for him he collapsed just before the gate, totally unconscious. When the ambulance arrived, the medics found the cable, removed it and eventually brought him round no worse for his experience. But when the management got the gatekeeper's report on the incident, he was sacked: a heavy price to pay for a small length of cable.

It never ceased to amaze me the lengths men would go to in order to get something for nothing, without being caught. One very serious theft took place at night on one of the liners being built. The ship was nearing its completion completely fitted out with all carpets, curtains, soft furnishings, etc. except for one lounge where the carpet was rolled up waiting to be fitted. It was during the night shift that the carpet was lifted, taken to the ship's side where it was lowered onto a small motor launch never to be seen again. The police never found the culprits and it cost the yard a lot of money to replace, for it was a huge carpet which probably would have covered thirty ordinary house lounges. The theft had been carefully planned and would have made quite a bit of money for those responsible when cut up into manageable sizes and sold. This type of carpet was of the finest quality and the most expensive to buy.

It was after this incident that a yard detective was employed to organise a small staff to patrol the ships, particularly when they were near the completion stage. This still did not deter some of the men, who would take light fittings, switches, irons, soap holders, toilet roll holders, mats, etc. Anything they could remove easily went, even though the electrical equipment they were taking would not work on their house electrical supply. In the end, the ship's trade foreman used to have to make sure that all completed cabins and rooms were locked and only authorised personnel allowed into them. Theft within the yard obviously cost the company dearly.

There were times when we were allowed to buy certain redundant items. These items were usually purchased from a store at the rear of the joiners shop. The best time to visit this store was just after one of the liners had sailed from the yard, for that's when there would be quite a variety of redundant material to buy at a very low price. There was anything from wood, Formica, chrome taps, stainless steel coat hooks and soap dishes. I knew colleagues who lined their bathrooms out with plain or patterned Formica left over from a ship and very smart and efficient they turned out to be.

Of course there was always one who wanted more than what was on offer. He would steal whatever wood he wanted then purchase enough redundant wood to cover up the stolen pieces, then hand his purchase pass into the gatehouse who were none the wiser as he left the yard. Having said that, the management eventually caught on to what was happening and stopped all purchasing of materials by the staff. The greed of one spoilt it for the majority.

11. Shipyard Ladies

ALTHOUGH THE WORKERS in the yard were predominantly men, there were quite a large number of women. They were aged anywhere between twenty and sixty. Their main task was to sweep and clean up any mess created by the workmen in all compartments and deck areas throughout the fitting out stage of the ship. Also in the ship's completion stage they had to wash, clean, dust and polish all compartments ready for final owner's inspection.

Some of these women were hard and rough characters coming from one of the tough areas of the neighbourhood and they needed to be tough with some of the men they had to work with. As you can imagine, there was some great patter between the workmen and the cleaners, not to mention the swearing and suggestive remarks. There was also the flirting between the younger ones, for some of the women were very attractive and it wasn't unknown for one of the workmen and one of the cleaners to be seen disappearing into a cabin on their own to enjoy the delights of unrestrained passion. Many is the time I've seen the foreman banging on the door of a cabin trying to get a couple out and back to work. "What a spoil sport!" was the cry from all around.

Some of the older and wiser women were friendly and kind, particularly to us young apprentices. They sort of mothered us and took care of us, they even used to share their bait (sandwiches) with us.

There were some real characters amongst those women, who always had a smile and generally a kind word for everyone, even though their language could be rough at times. One older woman working close by to me had a young daughter also working on the ship. One day the daughter decided to go off with one of the workmen into one of the cabins for a little 'physical wrestling' but unfortunately her mother found out what she was doing. She just about broke the cabin door down with her brush, amidst obscenities shouted at the workman who was obviously by now too frightened to open the door. When the door was eventually opened and they came out, the mother chased the offending 'wooer' with her brush flaying at him and mouthing the most offensive bad language you could imagine, as he ran along the deck and eventually off the ship. The daughter didn't fare much better once her mother returned. We young apprentices certainly had our eyes opened to life in a shipyard.

12. Wartime

At home we were all very much aware of the regular air raids taking place. For safety during an air raid we had an Anderson shelter which was made out of galvanised steel, half buried into the ground with the top semi-circular part of it protruding out of the ground but covered in earth to disguise it. My father fitted it out with wooden seats right round the perimeter and made it as comfortable as possible for our family and two neighbours who shared the shelter with us.

My father was given the honour of being air raid warden for our street and was given a grey painted helmet, a fire bucket and a stirrup pump for the quenching of any fire. I was quite proud as a young boy that my father was given this important position, however I cannot imagine how one stirrup pump could put out the fire in a house that had been bombed. With the shelter being buried so deep into the garden, there was a tendency for water to gather each day in the base of the shelter, so two large holes were dug, one at each end to allow the water to drain into them. It was my responsibility to bail out the water each day before going to school. This really made me feel important and with a father holding the position of a warden, I was the envy of my street pals.

There were some heavy bombing raids on Tyneside. One of the worst was when a direct hit was made on a large warehouse close to Newcastle city centre. When the explosion took place it made our air raid shelter, which was two and a half miles away, move. We were all scared that night. The blaze at the warehouse lasted well over a week for it contained vast amounts of sugar, fats, bacon and many other inflammable products.

If the 'all clear' siren sounded to signal the end of an air raid after midnight, then we youngsters were given the morning off school. I often prayed for the raid to continue after midnight!

Wartime in the shipyard was pretty dangerous at times due to the constant air-raids carried out by the Germans. I was only a boy at the time but I can vividly remember some of the air-raids that took place.

'Jerry' as the Germans were known, was after sinking some of the warships being built in the yard, two in particular were their target, a battleship and an aircraft carrier being built at the same time. Early one morning I had just come downstairs at home and about to have my breakfast before heading off to school when there was a very unusually loud sound of an approaching aeroplane. My mother was just opening the curtains at that time and shouted for me to come to the window and see this aeroplane which appeared to be flying just above the surrounding houses. The plane was so low you could see the outline of the pilot in the cockpit. Mother thought it was one of our planes until she recognised the German swastika insignia emblazoned on the body of the aircraft. I was immediately pulled away from the window and quickly escorted to the air raid shelter along with my younger sister, Sylvia. The rest of the family by this time had gone to work.

This incident, we found out later culminated in a German bomber plane having somehow slipped through the British defence system early that morning, headed for the Naval Yard and unloaded his bombs, hoping to hit the battleship which was berthed alongside the big crane. Fortunately the bombs missed the ship but one landed right at the base of one of the big cranes supporting uprights, buried half in and half out the ground, without exploding. The bomb was defused by the army bomb disposal team and then presented to the company who put it on display in the model room for all visitors to view.

On another occasion 'Jerry' dropped a bomb which appeared to miss its intended target but exploded and blew up the workmen's canteen. There were a few casualties but the fortunate thing was that if 'Jerry' had been ten minutes earlier, then there would have been a real disaster, for the canteen was full of men and women taking their tea break.

Some of the older tradesmen could remember during the war years when women used to work with the tradesmen, carrying out mainly labouring tasks. This pairing of male and female certainly helped the war effort with respect to there being a shortage of labour in the shipyards. It also caused a few broken marriages with the affairs that took place between working couples.

Night shift was the worst, they tell me, for the ships were nothing but glorified brothels at times and with little precautions available you can imagine the consequences of some of the relationships. However, the yards were still churning war ships out for the navy month after month. I reckon the presence of women on board the ships boosted the moral of everyone and thereby increased production. (That is shipyard production, not babies!)

One of my older colleagues who had worked during the war, remembered one disaster which occurred when they were building submarines. Apparently the yard had just about completed building the hull of one of the many submarines being built at that time, when the wooden shores supporting her collapsed, leaving the whole structure lying on its side alongside the keel blocks. Fortunately the supports were not very high so there was little damage to the structure of the submarine but the big problem was getting the submarine back onto the launchways. Two heavy duty cranes came to the rescue eventually, although a good deal of precious time was lost on the build programme to rectify the accident.

Shipyard work at most times can be dangerous but during the war it must have been quite a nightmare, particularly when the air raid siren blew and you knew some German bomber was on his way ready to drop his load of bombs on you. There were amusing incidents which took place during the war at the shipyard. One of my colleagues from the drawing office, a chap called George Hume, told me about an incident he had experienced while working on a submarine which was being fitted out alongside one of the yard jettys.

Now George was small in stature, about five foot nothing, and fairly slim.

He had been working on one of the sub's torpedo tubes which required him to go inside head first, lying on his stomach about half way down the tube. After completing the task he was given, he found he could not get back out of the tube due to it being a very confined space and with the energy he had expended working, his body had naturally heated up and expanded, jamming him inside the torpedo tube. Obeying his cry for help, much effort was made to pull him out but to no avail. The harder they pulled the more he became stuck. Of course by this time George was sweating profusely which only made matters worse. Fortunately George was of a very placid nature and took everything calmly as one would expect.

There is, of course, always one joker on board no matter what happens and this particular one suggested that they fire George out of the tube. This jocular remark went down well with those observing the situation but not so with George who was now trying to relax and stay calm so that his body temperature would reduce and enable him to be pulled free. Eventually the tube was greased as far as possible up to George's body then they gently hosed his body with cold water. This did the trick, for George's body temperature dropped and he was eventually pulled free to cheers from those around.

I did say amusing incidents - the above was probably serious at the time, but in a shipyard, no matter how serious the event, someone will make fun of it or make some amusing remark to relieve the tension. George said that he really thought they would have to fire him out of the tube which he wasn't looking forward to as he couldn't swim! I can't think what work would be required to be done inside a torpedo tube, but George assured me that what had happened was true. Mind you, I can't help but smile when I think about the situation George was in that day although it wasn't very amusing for him.

Another incident, that was not so amusing, took place on one of the ship's gangways. When a ship was being fitted out alongside the jetty, there were normally two gangways linking the ship to the jetty, one positioned forward and one aft. At the approach of finishing time, between five or ten minutes, the majority of men would make their way to the gangway ready to leave the ship once the siren sounded. At the foot of the gangway would be the various trade foremen standing chatting about the morning events or how well Newcastle United had played over the weekend, although their real purpose was to see that no person left the ship before time. This particular day, as the time got nearer to twelve o' clock the men slowly eased their way onto the gangway and gradually moved further and further down until the front row could go no further without facing the wrath of one or more of the foremen. The men were absolutely crammed onto the gangway like sardines in a tin. Suddenly there was an almighty creaking and splintering of wood. The gangway broke and collapsed into the river with about twenty or thirty men following it. There was absolute pandemonium as people rushed to help get the men out of the water. A number of life-belts and lengths of rope were thrown to those now struggling to stay afloat, in particular those who could not swim and those who had injured themselves after they had fallen.

As I recall, there were no fatal injuries or anyone drowned, but all had to be taken to hospital, some to receive treatment for their wounds and all to be inoculated against the polluted water they had swallowed. This incident taught the management a lesson as far as safety was concerned, and from then on all gangways were made out of steel.

13. Refreshment and Travel

IT WAS ABOUT THE END OF MY FIRST YEAR working on the ships that the management decided to introduce tea breaks after much pressure by the trade unions within the yard. We were allowed a ten minute break in the morning at 9.00am then ten minutes in the afternoon at 3.00pm. These official breaks were meant to stop all the unofficial ones and it mainly achieved that except that there were still those who took advantage of the system and spent more than the ten minutes allotted. These were usually those who made their tea in a can as by this time the majority of workers were now using the modern thermos flask. There was still the old game of the management trying to catch workmen having a break outside the allotted time but in the main, most workmen stuck to the time schedule.

At finishing times there was always what can only be described as a stampede for the canteen. From the ships, workshops and stocks, men raced each other to reach the canteen first. It was the survival of the fittest, for there was always about twenty or more of the fit apprentices in the lead. That is until they got to the entrance which only permitted two at a time, so you can imagine the scrambling and fighting that went on to get through the door first. Then sometimes when the tradesmen arrived they would order the apprentices to the back of the queue amidst a lot of groans and swearing.

I mainly went home for my dinner (there was no such thing as lunch in those days) though occasionally I did use the canteen. Canteen meals were plain wholesome meals, no frills, good old mince and dumplings, pot-pie, sausage and mash and delicious puddings like spotted dick and custard, ginger sponge and jam roly-poly, all with custard. Mind, you had to be alert whilst eating your dinner for you would always get someone trying to distract your attention whilst his mate stole half your food. Then there would be the wag, who would pour salt in your glass of water when you were not looking.

One day, there was an almighty uproar in the canteen when one man accused another of stealing meat of his plate. The accused saw red and poured his dinner over the other whose mate in turn retaliated by throwing his dinner back at the accused, missed him and hit someone further down the table. This then set off a chain reaction whereby the whole table of twenty workmen joined in throwing dinner and pudding at each other. It was like something out of a comedy film. Eventually they ran out of food, stopped, sat down, food dripping from them, saw the state of each other and burst out laughing, much to the relief of those watching, who thought there was going to be a nasty punch-up. In the end Geordie humour prevailed.

Racing up to the canteen was tame compared with finishing time at the yard. Particularly, at the Swan Hunter yard where I finished up working. The yard entrance was at the bottom of a steep bank and consisted of a steel roller - shutter type gate. Just before the buzzer sounded, there would be anywhere between five hundred to over a thousand men behind the gate waiting to run up the bank and catch a bus home. When the buzzer sounded, the roller shutter would slowly rise and as it did so several bodies would roll out beneath, scramble to their feet and shoot off up the bank as though the devil were after them. How on earth some of them did not get trampled no-one will ever know but there were some very near misses. The worst part was when the buzzer sounded for the men to enter the yard. The buzzer used to sound at about ten minutes before the gates were due to close then it would sound again at one minute to starting time and continue to sound until the official starting time was reached. Then the buzzer would cease and the roller shutter would slowly come down. The stragglers coming down the bank would have to start running to get under the shutter before it closed. However the last few left it a little too late and finished up doing a limbo dance beneath the gate as it got to about three feet off the ground. I've even seen them crawling under to get into work on time, for if you were locked out, you then had to enter the yard by the gate-house where your name was recorded and a quarter of an hour's money deducted off your wages. It was a miracle that no one was squashed beneath the entrance gate. At the time it was quite amusing watching all these men ducking, limbo'ing and rolling beneath the gate.

About half a mile from the yard was the bus terminus where, at five o'clock at night, there would be a fleet of trolley buses waiting to transport the shipyard workmen back home. Watching the men boarding the buses was an education, for they would arrive at the bus stop and stand in an orderly queue until the bus moved off from its parking space and pulled up at the stop. Then all hell was let loose. The orderly queue disappeared and it was a case of every man for himself. Everyone surged forward, all trying to get on the bus at once, hence there were times nobody moved because they were jammed between the entrance pole and the back of the bus. Then when the conductor thought there were enough passengers on, he would ring the bell instructing the driver to move off. The bus would move off with men still jumping on clinging precariously to the bus boarding pole, some falling off either losing their grip or failing to keep their feet on the platform. In those days by law, there were only five people allowed to stand downstairs on the bus. That did not apply to the shipyard workers' buses where there would be ten or more standing, as well as those on the platform. It was no good the conductor instructing them to get off, for he would then be met with verbal abuse. Sometimes the driver would come to the assistance of the conductor and refuse to move the bus until the platform was cleared of bodies. Sometimes it worked, other times, as soon as the driver got into his cab, the men would jump back onto the platform.

Patience was not a shipyard worker's attribute. It was laughable really because it seemed that everyone wanted to be on that first bus, when there were plenty of empty ones behind.

14. Fear and Danger

DURING THEIR CONSTRUCTION, ships can be dangerous in some areas. More so during the early days of construction when the ship is just a steel shell with little or no machinery fitted on board. During this period main power cables are run throughout the ship supplying the various sections and departments which have electrical equipment fitted.

I was working on staging right at the top of the engine room casing helping my 'marker off', a chap called Jimmy Topping, to plan and mark out the route of some main cables. We were standing on two nine inch wide planks of wood which were placed alongside each other and which stretched across to the other side of the engine room with a void and a drop beneath us of about 60ft down to the engine room floor. There was I, clinging desperately to the bulkhead of the casing, whilst little Jimmy, who was only 5ft, was walking back and forth across these planks from one side of the engine casing to the other without any fear at all. What made it worse was every time he walked across the planks they would shake and wobble as one of the planks was slightly warped and this just made me more terrified. I've never liked heights since.

One day the foreman electrician asked me to go up the mast to replace a lamp that had burnt out. I refused, saying I was nervous of heights. He replied that it was part of my apprenticeship training and that I must carry out the task. I went and got the replacement lamp from the store and reluctantly went back on board the vessel. I must have stood looking at the top of the mast light fitting for some considerable time thinking what a long way up it was and then deciding that there was no way that I was going up that mast. Just then one of my colleagues came along and asked what was wrong. On hearing my predicament, he immediately volunteered to do the task for me. I was so pleased, I even offered him a couple of bob (two old shillings) for his efforts but he would not hear of such a thing. A true colleague and friend without a doubt.

The next day, the foreman said that he was pleased that I'd carried out the task, and knew I could do it. Little did he know. After this incident I was always wary when joining a new ship where he was the foreman, in case I was asked to perform what seemed to me to be a trapeze act.

Apart from having a fear of heights, I was also claustrophobic and it was on board one ship that was nearing completion that I experienced my worst nightmare. I was working in the engine room at the time when I was requested, or should I say, ordered, to go down into the double bottom of the ship to do some work on what I recall was the ship's echo sounder. At this point I think I should explain just what the double bottom comprises. It is the space between the outer steel skin on the bottom of a ship and the watertight plating over the bottom deck or floor of the ship. A double bottom serves two purposes, first as a protection against disaster when the outer bottom shell is holed by running aground or striking some unseen object in the sea and second as a convenient stowage for liquid ballast. The double bottom was comprised of numerous structural supporting frames and girders each of which having holes in them just large enough for a man to crawl through, so making it a very enclosed and cramped area.

The entrance into this space was via a manhole cut into the floor plate, just large enough to allow a man to pass through. I went down through the manhole into the gloomy double bottom, which was poorly lit by temporary lighting, and cautiously made my way through the vertical holes of the supporting frames on all fours, till I reached the echo sounder position. Having crawled to this position, I now had to crouch down into a most uncomfortable position and endeavour to connect up the cables. It was while I was squatting there rubbing my head to relieve the pain having hit it for the fourth time on the deck head within a couple of minutes, that it came to my mind that only the 'marker off' knew I was down there.

I started to imagine what would happen if the 'marker off' forgot I was down in the double bottom and someone saw the manhole uncovered and put the plate back over it. How would I get out? By this time I was starting to feel claustrophobic and started to panic, feeling hot and sweaty. I gathered myself together and decided to try and complete the task I was set as I didn't fancy having to return to do it the following day. The job was completed in record time, for I was now desperate to get out of this hot stuffy enclosure. I started to crawl back towards the manhole. Unfortunately I had lost my bearings and I didn't seem able to find the entrance and by this time I really was starting to panic. My mind was racing away thinking that the entrance plate would be bolted down in position and I would be left there to rot away as the 'marker off' had a memory lapse and could not remember anything.

Just as I was about to start shouting, a voice suddenly shouted "are you alright down their, big fella?". It was 'Bomber'. He had been instructed to keep an eye on me while I was in the double bottom. What a relief. I was out of that confined space in double quick time much to his amusement when I told him what had happened. Later, due to new safety rules, no one was allowed in the double bottom without someone stood by the manhole entrance to keep in contact with them.

I cannot emphasise enough the dangers present during the construction of a ship and the need to be aware of what is going on around you at all times. One day while I was working close to the top of the engine room, one of the jetty crane jibs swung over the top of the engine room skylight to lower a large section of steel grating which was used for the walkways in the machinery space. I recall someone shouting "Look out below!", then suddenly the grating fell from the crane into the bowels of the engine room. It was sometime later that I was told a labourer had been hit by the falling grating and had died. Apparently he had not heard the warning and it had landed on his head. There was an enquiry into the whole incident but as no one was specifically to blame,

I understand the company paid compensation to the family of the deceased. It was a sad day, not only for the family but also for his work colleagues, in fact those working on that particular vessel went home as a token of respect.

Once again, safety rules and regulations were tightened and enforced to make the yard a safer place to work. Of course you still got those who took short cuts and risked the safety of others.

15. Paddy

NEXT TO A GEORDIE there are no friendlier folks other than perhaps the Irish and we had quite a few working in the yard at the time. Originally when the yards were first built, almost all of the heavy labouring work was carried out by what was known in those days as Irish navvies. They did all the hard digging of the bank-side and clearing of the site to make way for the launchway jetties, etc which enabled the yard to be constructed. It must have been back breaking work although I'm informed they were big strong men who worked hard, played hard and drank gallons. Many a fight outside 'The Stack', the local pub, was started by a 'Paddy', as Irishmen were known locally. Invariably though they were very friendly and good humoured joking about themselves.

It was on one of the tankers we were fitting out at the time that I became acquainted with Paddy, the electrician's labourer, who one can only describe as being one of the so called 'little people' from Ireland. He was five foot nothing with his boots on and bald so he always wore a cap pulled down one side at a jaunty angle which made him look impish just like an Irish gnome. Although he was small, Paddy made up for his lack of height with his mouth, for he had a voice like a foghorn. He did not talk, he shouted. The only redeeming feature about this was his Irish accent and his love for telling funny stories.

Paddy was a hard worker and no task was too difficult for him, for although small, he was as strong as an ox. He was assigned to work for Alfie Fairbairn, an electrician's 'marker off' who I happened to be working with at that time. Hence I got to know Paddy very well. I don't know what it was but I always seemed to get on well with the little people, perhaps it was because I was a very quiet person or maybe it was just that I was a good listener. I certainly had to be with Paddy around.

Paddy told me he was born in Dublin and his father brought the family over to England in the late 1920's looking for work as there was none in Ireland, particularly if you were labouring. After a short period of labouring in the Liverpool docks, the family eventually moved to Tyneside where Paddy's father got a job in the shipyard. Paddy reckoned that it was his father's hard work in the yard that got him his first job. Management probably thought 'like father like son'. Sure enough, they were right, for Paddy turned out to be as hard a worker as his father. Working with Paddy you never had a dull moment and 'bait' time couldn't come quick enough for me for that's when Paddy would tell the tale. He never failed to make you laugh - even the simplest of tales were amusing.

One morning tea break as he was pouring his tea out of his flask (no common tea can for Paddy), he said "Ken, did you know, there has been a nasty accident in the yard, this morning?" "No", said I, in all seriousness whereupon Paddy began to relate what had happened. An Irish friend of his called Sean who worked in the fitters shop had got too near a cutting machine and unfortunately got his right ear cut off. Unfortunately the ear had been thrown somewhere onto the workshop floor when sliced off. The foreman immediately ordered everyone in the shop to look for the ear for he said that the sooner they find the ear the more chance the doctor would have of sewing it back in place. By this time I was all ears. After a couple of minutes, one chap shouted out "is this your ear Sean?" Sean looked at the ear carefully and said "no it is not," The Foreman just about blew his top, he said "what do you mean it's not your ear?". Sean replied, "Well mine had a pencil behind it!" Need I say more, typical Paddy humour.

Paddy was also a marksman with the catapult. When the job couldn't be progressed because of some delay in materials or other trades falling behind schedule it was time for target practice. Paddy, some of the other apprentices and I, would each make a catapult out of an unused welding rod by bending it into a 'Y' shape and tying a length of electrician's rubber sheath taken from some scrap cable onto each tip of the 'Y' section. When the catapult was fully stretched it was lethal, for it could fire a quarter inch steel nut about twenty yards (18 metres). Mind you, we never fired at our fellow workmen. The catapults came out when the tide was out and the ship was lying low in the water. In this situation some of the ship's port holes would be below the jetty which was built on huge timber stilts projected at an angle and fastened into a sloping concrete base which was revealed when the tide went out.

Now when the tide was out, that was the signal for all the yard rats to appear under the jetty scampering around all over the concrete base looking for any food which may have been left by the lowering tide. This was the time for some target practice. Each of us would select a porthole and commence firing our ammunition of steel nuts at the rats. Every time a rat was hit a cheer would go up after which each would claim that it was his firing that had hit the rat but invariably it would be Paddy's firing that had found the target. Some of the rats would not always be killed by the steel nuts. It depended where it was hit. Anywhere on the leg or body would only maim it but if got hit on the head then it was fatal. Some thought this target practice a bit cruel but it certainly kept the number of rats down and to Paddy and the rest of us it was good fun.

Rats in the shipyard were a menace for they would eat their way through anything so much so that the management used to hire a rat catcher to come into the yard on a Saturday afternoon when it was quiet. Apart from laying traps in some of the awkward places, the rat catcher would rely on his little terrier dog to chase and kill most of the rats but really he was fighting a losing battle for they bred quicker than he could kill them. However he did keep the number down. The most important feature with respect to eliminating the rats was to make certain they did not get on board the ships. There were two ways in which the rats could get on board and that was either up the gangway or up the rope or metal mooring ropes holding the vessel alongside the fitting-out jetty. The rats never seemed to bother with the gangways as there were always workmen around but they did attempt to get on board via the mooring ropes. However they were prevented from doing so by a thin metal disc about twelve inches (30 centimetres) in diameter fitted half way up and around each mooring rope tethered to the ship. This stopped the rats in their tracks.

Paddy came in one morning and said to me, "My luck's right out just now Ken, I've lost a packet on the horses, I've had me car pinched and me laddie's broken his leg". "How's that for bad luck". "That's nothing" said I, "I bought a new suit with three pairs of trousers. Two days later I burnt a hole in the jacket pocket". That was bad luck.

16. Tests and Trials

Y SECOND YEAR as an apprentice working on the ships became a little more interesting, for I was now given tasks to do on my own, even though these were the simpler ones within the trade. We apprentices used to have competitions between each other to see who could finish their allotted task first. The tasks of course were the same which usually involved completely wiring a cabin. This competitiveness meant the job got done much quicker than normal although it was not always correct, much to the annoyance of the 'marker off' who checked the work. He often found that the cabin door switch operated the bathroom light, the bathroom door switch operated the bed light and the bed light switch turned the shower on, etc. He regularly emphasised, in typical shipyard language, that none of us would make a good electrician. Nevertheless, the competition went on.

The cabins used to be wired out with lead covered cable which were neatly clipped together side by side then polished over with a rag until they were shining. This was a complete waste of time because invariably they were painted over but we apprentices thought it looked good and would get us in the 'marker off's good books, however to no avail.

The most rewarding period of working on a ship was when it was close to its completion date, for then most of the equipment and systems would be ready for testing. There was no greater satisfaction than to see a piece of equipment or system operating smoothly, some small part of which you had contributed to. There was a feeling of excitement just before the test on a piece of equipment or system began, particularly if it was the main engines or generators being run for the first time.

Most of the vessels were driven by steam turbine engines. It was later that diesel engines became the preferred method of propulsion. I remember being allowed to watch one test on a steam turbine engine during the course of which the engine, for no apparent reason, started to slow down. It was soon detected that the steam pressure supply from the boilers was dropping. Standing alongside me was a young apprentice fitter and his charge hand who, on seeing what had happened to the engine, began to explain to the apprentice what was wrong and how to remedy the problem. I was all ears ready to learn all I could when the charge hand told the apprentice that the engine required more steam and that he (the apprentice) should go to the boiler room and get a bucket of steam from one of the boilers. The apprentice duly toddled off to do as he was told, much to the amusement of those close by, including myself who was now a second year apprentice and hopefully could not be taken in by such pranks anymore.

The apprentice returned with a bucket with a lid on it and related to the charge-hand that the boiler room could only let them have half a bucket of steam, would that be alright? After the laughter had died down, I could not decide whether the apprentice had got his own back with his snappy 'half bucket' response or whether he was as gullible as the charge hand made him out to be. I must mention that those carrying out the test weren't very pleased with the hilarity going on around them and threatened to have those responsible removed from the engine room, for the testing of equipment and systems was not the time for pranks. But pranks were part of a young lad's apprenticeship.

Another big event in the completion of a ship is the sea trials, when the vessel is taken out to sea to commence her trials, generally off the north east coast. This constitutes a very extensive period of tests and trials of certain pieces of the ship's equipment, particularly the engines, generators and bridge navigation equipment, including test runs on the 'measured mile' just north of Alnmouth. This was where the ship was put to test to see if she would achieve her proposed speed and performance over the measured mile. Of course there were other tests being carried out while the speed trials were going on such as recording vibration figures in various sections of the ship while the engines were at maximum designed speed. Anyone who thought going on sea trials was a 'jolly' got a rude awakening for the trials programme went on all day and night, anywhere from three to five days or more depending on the length of programme and the complexity of the vessel.

Sea trials was one event I longed to participate in but it was very rare that apprentices got the chance to go. It wasn't till many years later that my opportunity came. It wasn't everyone's ambition to go on sea trials because some were very bad sailors. I've heard it said that some workmen were seasick before the ship had reached the mouth of the river which at most times was flat calm. There were some sea trials during which the weather was extremely rough. Consequently most of the trial's party were seasick. The owner's representatives preferred rough weather for it was ideal to witness the performance of the vessel in extreme conditions. While a few men flatly refused to go on trials because of seasickness, others would put up with this discomfort because they knew that come pay day, their wage packet would be greatly enhanced with the extra allowances paid for attending the sea trials.

Sometimes sea trials caused quite a bit of animosity amongst the work force - generally from those who were never selected to go - against the ones who were regularly picked and all because of the extra money to be gained. I have to admit it did seem a little unfair at times. However from the company's point of view, all they wanted was the right men to carry out a very important task.

17. A Change of Course

I was well into my second year's apprenticeship now doing small jobs on my own but nothing really exciting or satisfying. Winter was here, it was cold, starting and finishing times were dark and wet, there were no pranks or funny stories being exercised or told. I was also working on a ship that had not long been launched. Hence, it was cold steel everywhere and everything you touched numbed your fingers, not to mention that you had to keep on the move to keep your feet from turning numb. Then, when the working day was finished, I would go home, get washed, have my tea, then have to set off for evening classes which lasted for two and a half hours. By the time I got back home and had my supper it was time to go to bed. What made things worse was that I was going out with a nice blonde called Joan Lillie, a local girl I met at the church youth club and I much preferred her company than going to night classes.

As you can gather, I was getting really depressed, not about Joan, but with my job and night classes, the cold, the wet, the early rising and the late finishing, all I had to look forward to was the weekend. I really felt that my working life was not as happy as it seemed the previous year, so it was in this state of mind that I decided to change my job.

One Saturday morning I caught the local bus and went to Pilgrim Street police station to see if I could become a policeman. I had previously thought about joining the police force due to the fact some people I met always implied that I should have been a policeman with being so tall. Well, there I was standing at the reception desk feeling a little apprehensive as to what I was going to let myself in for. The reception constable greeted me with a smile and asked how he could help me? I told him I would like to join the police force. "Well you're the right height for the job if nowt else" was his reply bearing in mind that you had to be at least six foot (180 cms.) to join the police force in those days. I thought to myself, well, that's one qualification I've passed. Then came the bombshell, he asked me if I'd done my national service. National service, for those of you who are too young to remember, was a period of two years service in either one of the three armed forces which had to be served by every young man between the age of eighteen and twenty three years. The reason for the age range is that you could apply to be deferred from entering service if you were working on Ministry of Defence or essential government work up to a maximum age limit of twenty three years.

In answer to the desk constable's question I had to say no, as I was still only seventeen. "Come back when you've done your national service son, then we will consider your application" was his advice. I left the police station feeling absolutely gutted for I had fully expected to be accepted as a police recruit, if not immediately, then certainly within a few weeks.

Of course I had forgotten all about national service which could not be avoided. I went home to think about what I was going to do about my career having found out that I could not join the police force until I was at least eighteen years old. I realised that there were three options open to me. First, to do my national service as soon as I reached the age of eighteen, after which, join the police force. The second option was to continue to serve my apprenticeship as an electrician until I qualified at the age of twenty one, then carry out my national service duties thereby enabling me to join the police force when I reached the age of twenty three. The third option was to forget about the police force, carry on with my apprenticeship and see if I could develop and improve my career within the shipyard.

After weighing-up the options and seeking the advice of my previous boss Mr. MacCallum, I decided the second option would be the most sensible as it gave me the opportunity to qualify as an electrician thereby enabling me to at least have a trade to revert to if I did not like the police force. I must say Mr. MacCallum asked me to think long and hard about changing my career at such an early stage of my life although he did emphasise that it was no good staying in a job you did not like. Now that I reflect on that period of time, I don't think I really disliked shipyard work, it was just a build-up of unpleasant circumstances at that time. I soon forgot about how miserable I'd been and set about my tasks with more enthusiasm. This was probably due to the fact that I now had a goal to achieve.

18. The Big Fight

ONE OF MY FELLOW APPRENTICES at this time was a lad called Jimmy Hornby. Jimmy was slightly older than me, he was short and podgy and had a fiery temper although he and I got on well together. Jimmy's father owned the local newspaper shop just outside the shipyard so every shipyard worker used to buy their paper or cigarettes from his shop - it was a little gold mine.

Getting back to Jimmy, although he was rough and tough at times, he spoke in a quiet, gentle type of voice which belied his true nature. If Jimmy did not like you, then as far as he was concerned, you were his enemy and if you tried to argue with him then that was an invite to fight him. He would find any excuse to start a fight. Size or weight did not matter, he would take anybody on and generally came out on top, mainly because he had no fear and went into a fight with both fists flaying continuously, irrespective of any blows he himself might suffer. His reputation as a fighter, or perhaps I should say as a bully, was well known throughout the shipyard. One day he got into an argument with a big strapping boilermaker. Jimmy wanted to fight him there and then but the boilermaker declined and said he did not want to lose his job by fighting on board the ship but would willingly fight Jimmy on the green just outside the shipyard gates. Jimmy, restrained by a few of his cronies from rushing into a fight, reluctantly agreed to the proposal, providing the fight took place in the dinner hour that day, at half past twelve.

As you can imagine, word got round the yard very quickly and soon there was a bookie taking bets on the result of the fight. Come lunchtime those who ate at the canteen dashed there to gulp down their dinners, then sped up to the top of the bank to get a good viewing position. Those who went home for dinner, including myself, ran all the way home and back within the half-hour we had available, before the Big Fight. I remember my mother remarking on the fact that I would get indigestion if I did not eat more slowly. I made some excuse for the rush but did not dare tell her the real reason for she abhorred men fighting and I know now that she would have been very surprised to know that I was going to watch such a fight. When I got back to the bankside where the fight was to take place, there was a huge crowd – a hundred or more. Someone had organised the crowd to form a huge circle making quite a large arena for the two fighters. The bookie by this time was very busy taking last minute bets on the offer of 4-1 on Geordie the boilermaker and 2-1 on Jimmy the apprentice electrician. It was now nearing half past twelve and you could feel the growing tension in the crowd. It was just as though two professional boxers were about to fight. Everyone was positioning to get the best view. I was near the back of the crowd but with being so tall had a fairly unrestricted view.

Geordie and Jimmy arrived spot on twelve thirty, the crowd parted to let them through, Jimmy went over to one side of the circle and Geordie over to the other. Both were wearing their boiler suits and work boots. The Bookie shouted out that the book was now closed and no more bets, he then blew a whistle which was the signal for the fight to begin and for the crowd to start shouting and encouraging their prospective winner. As soon as that whistle blew Jimmy was off his mark immediately to meet Geordie with his usual style of flaying arms aimed at Geordie's head. The first few connected before Geordie could compose himself but then he started to get his punches in on Jimmy. It was anybody's guess, after five minutes of the bloodiest fight witnessed, as to who was going to win. Geordie had the edge on strength of punches, but Jimmy landed more punches. By this time, remember, there were no rounds or rest, it was a continuous fight to the finish, both fighter's noses were bleeding, there was blood all over their boiler suits, they were both starting to show complete exhaustion and were both a bloody mess. This was when I decided I'd seen enough and was just about to depart when a voice from the crowd shouted that the police were on their way. This was the signal for the fight to cease and the crowd to move off back inside the yard to their respective work stations. I heard later that Jimmy and Geordie were rushed away down to the yard toilets where they were cleaned up as best as they could be. By the time the police arrived most of the crowd had returned to work and the fighters were safely inside the yard. It was a wasted journey as far as the police were concerned. No one had won the battle. There were a few workmen in the crowd who would have stopped the fight if they could but would not dare. If they had stepped inside that circle there was the fear of being hit by one of the fighters or being attacked by the crowd, most of whom were enjoying the gory scene before them. That afternoon I felt sick at the thought of what I had witnessed and was disgusted with myself for being part of it. Another lesson I learnt, don't follow the crowd. I think Jimmy learnt his lesson too; that you can't resolve your differences successfully by fighting and bullying people, for I never saw or heard of him fighting again.

19. Race Week

Winter was over and warmer weather was on the way, as we entered the month of June. The warmer weather always cheered the workmen. It was a blessing for the management, for production always increased when the weather was fine. For me the best thing about June was that this was the month we took our first week's holiday. Apart from the statutory holidays of Christmas, Easter and Bank holidays, we only got two weeks holiday per year. The first week had to be taken on Race Week which was the second last week in June. The second week's holiday was the last week of July or the first week in August, taken alternate years, to avoid all the shipyards being off together. Race Week on Tyneside was very special for that was the week the annual Temperance Fair was held on the Newcastle town moor. This was the biggest travelling fair in Europe and drew record crowds from all over the county. Race Week was also famous for, as the name implies, horse racing took place at Gosforth Park race course all of that week. The highlight of the racing calendar for that week was the 'Northumberland Plate' race, better known to Geordies as 'The Pitman's Derby'. This race used to take place on a Saturday afternoon which was ideal for families to have a day out together.

The whole family would go into Newcastle to do shopping, have some lunch, then dad would go off to the races while mother and the kids would go up to the town moor to have a look around the fair ground and sample some of the roundabouts and side-shows. This was the highlight of the holiday week for many shipyard and pitmen's families. Most families stayed at home the holiday week, mainly because they could not afford to go away. If the weather was fine, holiday enjoyment for the kids was a couple of trips on the local train down to Tynemouth, Cullercoats or Whitley Bay beaches for the day. Mother would pack sandwiches for dinner which were invariably soggy egg and tomato eaten on the beach. There was nothing nicer than eating sandwiches on the beach with the wind blowing from the northeast. Egg and tomato sandwiches tasted much nicer with a sprinkling of sand between them. Nobody seemed to mind for everyone was enjoying a sunny day, playing on the golden sand, building sandcastles, paddling in the sea and eating ice-cream cornets. Who needed the Costa Brava or the Algarve, it was all here on the Northumberland coast. Mind having said that, there were quite a few years when it poured with rain the whole of Race Week, which developed a reputation for being wet. Of course a visit to the fair always demanded the wearing of 'mack's and wellies', otherwise you got covered in clarts.

With this early annual holiday per year, the shipyard and other local factory workers and their families needed fine weather on race week but as we all know you can't order the weather you want. I recall that well loved Geordie comedian, Bobbie Thompson saying, "Ye shud niver have to gan back to wark straight afta a holida", ("You should never have to go back to work straight after a holiday") He was right. Monday morning in the shipyard after the Race Week holiday was somewhat different mainly because nobody felt like working. Most people stood around reminiscing about their holiday. It was only when the foremen or managers came on board that any real work was started. Roll on our next holiday.

20. Change

LIFE WAS BEGINNING to feel good again in the yard. I suppose it was the culmination of a few things, namely I had been moved from working on tankers to a refrigerated cargo ship for the City Line and I had a new marker-off and tradesman to work with. Not that there had been anything particularly wrong with my previous workmates or 'tanker' work, it was just that I found the refrigerated cargo ships much more interesting. I was progressing steadily as an apprentice and was doing well at the apprentice school and evening classes, although by this time I had given up my girlfriend. I went through a phase where I did not want to be tied down to one particular girl. I suppose I wanted to 'play the field' and anyway at this stage, I preferred the lads' company. Looking back now, I suppose I wanted the best of both worlds - and why not?

The ship I was now working on had refrigerated storerooms within the holds and these storerooms had wooden ducts around them where the cold air was ventilated out into the room. These ducts were made out of panelled timber and were accessible as there were various electrical controls and temperature equipment to be fitted in them. These ducts were just big enough for a normal size person to crawl into. No need to guess who got the job of wiring up the equipment in these refrigerated room ducts - yes - yours truly, the biggest fellow on the squad. It did not turn out to be too bad, although I got cramp a few times, but the worst thing was that it was very claustrophobic and there was always the chance that somebody would lock the entrance hatch without checking to see if anyone was inside. Memories of the manhole in the engine room double bottom.

The good thing about working in the ducts was that you could rest as much as you wanted without being seen for it was very rare that the foreman or managers ventured into such a tight space. Still, you had to keep an eye open for the marker-off checking on you. One afternoon I crawled along one of these ducts to my work station and instead of sitting in my hunched-up position I lay on my side at full stretch which was much more comfortable and promptly fell asleep. The next thing I remember was someone pulling at my ankles, it was the marker-off trying to wake me. He thought I'd passed out, fainted or something, and he was really worried until I woke up. Apparently I'd slept from half past one until four forty five. I'd missed hearing the three o'clock tea buzzer. Mind you, he gave me a real telling off once we were out of the duct. When asked why I was sleeping on the job, the only reply I could think of was that it must have been 'mince and dumplings day' and my mother had given me too big a dinner! He didn't fall for it, he said that was no excuse and that I should get to bed early or tell my mother to reduce her helpings. Fortunately he did not report me to the manager, otherwise I would have been in trouble. It's funny the events that stick in your mind.

My next assignment was working in the galley. This job, now that I look back, must have been the most unhealthy task I ever encountered in my apprenticeship. There I was standing on a joiner's stool clipping cables along a tray-plate attached to the deckhead with a welder close by whose welding arc was just about blinding me. Up above me in the galley uptake was a burner creating sparks which were falling all around me and a few yards away was a workman with a 'Terrazzo' floor polishing machine creating clouds of unhealthy dust. That was not all though, for on the other side was an insulation contractor fixing asbestos insulation sheets to the deckhead. So, there I was being blinded by welder's arc, burnt by sparks from the burner and breathing in tile and asbestos dust. Talk about health and safety at work, we did not know the meaning of the Act in those days. The fortunate thing about this little episode is that I was not in those unhealthy conditions for very long. Years later, some of my work colleagues' eyes deteriorated from constant welder's arc flashing and others eventually lost their life through asbestosis which is caused by inhaling the asbestos dust. This material is, of course, now banned. Conditions in those days were not very healthy to say the least.

21. Big Decisions

W E WERE NOW INTO AUTUMN and I was thinking to myself it won't be long before the cold winter days will be here with early dark cold mornings with snow and ice and freezing conditions on board ship. Not an experience to look forward to I must say. Then suddenly from the depths of despair in my day dreaming, I was summoned to go and see the head foreman electrician. I could not for the life of me think what I'd done wrong, unless the marker-off had told him about my sleeping on the job but that had happened over a week ago and if he had intended saying anything it would have been before now. So what could it be? It's strange how you always tend to think of the worst when you are summonsed to appear before the boss.

I duly arrived at his office, feeling a little apprehensive, knocked on the door then went in. "Ah Ken, come in and sit down". The expression on my face must have revealed my nervousness for he said "Relax, I'm not going to sack you. I've been talking to Mr. Birbeck in the electrical drawing office and he would like a good apprentice electrician to join his staff with a view to becoming a draughtsman and I've recommended you. How do you feel about it?" I was speechless for a minute, totally gobsmacked. My mind was in a whirl, I was not thinking straight. He must have realised my predicament for he told me to take some time to think about it but he needed to know by tomorrow night at the latest.

The five o' clock buzzer could not come quick enough for me that day as I couldn't concentrate on my work for thinking about the offer that had been made to me. Before going home I decided to call in at the main office and ask the advice of my old boss and friend Mr McCallum. He was delighted that the offer had been made to me for as far as he was concerned it was promotion within the company but emphasised that it had to be my decision. I told him about my intentions about joining the police force after doing national service although I appreciated that this offer was a good chance to further my career in shipbuilding. After a lengthy discussion and knowing that I could still change my career later if I wanted to, he convinced me that it would be a good move and was good experience for my future.

The following day I wasted no time in informing my head foreman of my decision to accept the offer and thanked him for giving me the opportunity of furthering my career. I was to start work in the drawing office the following Monday morning. I was so nervous, reporting to the chief electrical draughtsman on the Monday morning, it was like starting work again. I guess that no matter how often you change your job, the nervousness of starting afresh never ceases.

Tommy Birbeck, the chief electrical draughtsman, was another small man (it's funny how many small people played a part in my career). He was about five foot nothing, a little rotund around the girth, smartly dressed and was, as I later found out, a very fair and competent boss who was friendly and was prepared to enjoy a joke with his staff. His deputy was a chap called Joe McBride, a six footer, built like a barn door, totally different to Mr Birbeck but a likeable character who knew his job. The rest of the office comprised draughtsmen, apprentices, a male clerk and a female typist. I was assigned to work with a draughtsman named Billy White who happened to be a bachelor and who remained so for the rest of his life. He was one of the kindest, most gentle and unassuming men that I've met and a very good draughtsman. Bill and I became very good friends despite the wide age gap between us. One year we decided to go on holiday together to Majorca for a fortnight. This was to be a very big adventure for me as my holidays had always been spent at Costa del Hartlepool with my aunts or at home.

Bill and I could not go on holiday that year as I needed to save up which meant I had to put half a crown into the post office savings bank each week. I forget how much I actually saved but I do know there was enough to enjoy two weeks in the northern part of Majorca at a little bay called Puerto de Soller. It might seem strange in this day and age but Bill and I travelled all the way from Newcastle to Majorca by train and ferry, which took us two and a half days. For me, the travelling was all part of the holiday, experiencing long distance rail and ferry travel, seeing beautiful scenery and enjoying continental food. There was only one thing which marred the holiday and that was in the hotel we were staying were about twenty ex-wartime German officers each of whom had some form of disability either with their arms or legs. These disabilities had been incurred during the 1939-1945 war. Bill and I had tried all ways to get into conversation with them but it seemed as we were British they did not want to have anything to do with us and made that very plain by totally ignoring us.

The Hotel had its own private beach and as is custom, the Germans always managed to commandeer the best seats under the sun umbrellas. Then in the evenings in the lounge where entertainment was provided, it was always the Germans who took the front seats. Bearing in mind this was back in 1953, nothing changes, except that it's now with towels. Anyway, it did not really spoil our holiday for we made friends with a very nice couple from Lancashire.

One of the highlights of the holiday for me was swimming in the beautiful clear water around the island. Each morning we both donned a pair of goggles, a snorkel and flippers and set off swimming on the surface of the warm Mediterranean Sea. The reason I mention this is because when we decided to plan the holiday the year previously, I could not swim, so each morning of the working week, Bill and I used to attend Walker Baths at 7.30am where I would spend an hour learning to swim before going into work. By the end of the year I was quite competent at the breast stroke and swimming under water but I just couldn't get away with the crawl. Anyway the lessons enabled me to enjoy another very colourful underwater world in the Mediterranean Sea.

Back to the drawing office. The office comprised of long benches laid out in pairs, back to back with two or three draughtsmen and/or apprentices working each side. This meant that you could easily chat to the person opposite or turn and talk to the person behind you across the narrow alleyway that separated each pair of benches. The benches were positioned so that one end was placed up against the outside wall of the office which overlooked a grassy bank-side and the staff car-park. The other end of the bench stopped short of a half height wooden barrier on the other side of which was an alleyway. In the centre of the office was an area cordoned off by a wooden barrier where the deputy chief draughtsman and the office clerk worked. This was just outside the chief draughtsman's office alongside which was a small office for the use of the typist. At one end of the electrical drawing office was the tracing office and steel ordering department. At the other end was the naval architect's office and the printing room. On the opposite side of the building was the ship's drawing office which was responsible for the drawings of ship's steel work and 'fitting out' compartments, etc. In between the ship's drawing office and the electrical drawing office was a void area which covered the full height of the building and an area which housed a walk-in safe which covered about five floor levels. This safe housed a record of all plans and specifications of past and present built ships.

My first year in the drawing office was spent learning how to draw and print neatly in both pencil and ink. The pencil drawings and printing were done on white paper or manila which was a fairly stiff, buff coloured paper and the ink work carried out on a blue cloth material which had to have chalk rubbed over it before it would take the ink. This tracing cloth, as it was known, when washed out at home, made very good linen sheets, which could be used for making pillow cases, etc. or just used as dusters. Any spoilt tracing cloth was taken home where my mother made good use of it. After about a year working with Bill, I was designated to work with another senior draughtsman. This relocation took place every six months or so which enabled you to gain experience in the different sections of drawing office work and learn from the skills of each individual draughtsman.

By this time I was really enjoying working in the drawing office. It was a complete change to the shipyard. One of the advantages was that I now started work at 8.45am instead of 7.30am. Another advantage was that you worked in a healthier environment, although I did discover later on that the lighting in the office was very poor and I reckon that it was this poor lighting that contributed to my having to wear spectacles later in life.

Life in the drawing office was good, I enjoyed the work and with a lengthy lunch break and a fifteen minute tea break in the afternoon, who could wish for anything better? The afternoon tea breaks were taken in the staff canteen where we would all stand in an orderly queue to purchase our tea and cake. One afternoon I was standing in the queue patiently waiting my turn when the chap in front of me ordered tea, but nothing came out of the tea urn tap. The canteen lady serving the tea lifted the urn lid to see if it was empty. Apparently there was tea in the urn but there was something blocking the spout. The next thing I noticed was the tea lady with a pair of wooden tongs lifting from the boiler a dishcloth which someone had left inside when cleaning it out. Needless to say I passed on having tea that day.

One day I was sat at my bench directly opposite one of the older draughtsmen in the office when I noticed he had his chin resting on one hand with his elbow on the bench and his other hand holding a pencil with the point touching a drawing. It looked from a distance as though he was drawing, in actual fact he was fast asleep. This was a trick many of the older draughtsmen had learned over the years, you could appear to be working when you were asleep. There was one chap who could twitch his pencil every so often when asleep which made it appear more realistic to management that he was working. Mind you, many is the time the chief or his deputy would come up to the office to speak to them and they would jump at the shock, much to the amusement of the rest of the office. Fortunately there was no ill feeling, for I'm sure the chief and his deputy also sneaked naps when they thought no one could see them.

I worked with George Hume for a while on naval vessels; remember he was the one that got stuck up the torpedo tube during the war. Now that I was working on Ministry of Defence vessels I had to sign a secrecy declaration form which basically stated that I would not disclose any information to anyone outside the company with respect to my work on naval vessels. Now 'Big Brother' was watching me. George was a character. He never seemed to do much drawing work for he was always down the yard sorting problems out or sat at his bench repairing watches. However the tasks he was allocated were always completed on time. George sat right in the corner of the office directly in front of Mr Birbeck's office and next to the window. Fortunately for George he could not be seen by the chief draughtsman, as his lower office windows were frosted glass. This was probably the best position to be seated because you were well out of sight of the management. Also this was ideal for George to pursue his hobby of watch repairing and cleaning during working hours, although to be fair, he usually did most of it in his lunch break.

One afternoon everyone was going about their work as usual or at least appeared to be, for it was sleep time for some of the older ones, when all of a sudden, a very loud alarm bell began to ring waking the whole office up. Those who had been asleep jumped at the piercing sound. Most people after gathering their senses thought it was just a practice fire alarm going off and ignored it but those in the middle of the office realised it was coming from the corner where little George sat. However there was no sign of George. As I was the nearest, bearing in mind I worked with George, I went over to his bench to find out where the noise was coming from. It did not take long to find, for there standing right in the corner of his bench was the biggest alarm clock I'd ever seen with two huge bells each fitted at an angle of forty five degrees on the top of it making a horrendous noise. I picked the clock up endeavouring to find the lever that would kill the noise of the bells but to no avail. I scanned that clock closely to find the alarm off switch, but there did not seem to be one. After fumbling around without success one of my colleagues came over to see if he could silence it but he too failed. All the while this was going on these two bells were ringing away much to the annoyance of the office staff who were now shouting abusive remarks (to put it politely) at me. The only way to deaden the sound was to place a piece of rag underneath the two bell covers thereby jamming the mechanical hammers. By this time Joe MacBride, the assistant chief draughtsman, had turned up to see what all the noise was about. When he saw the alarm clock he exclaimed in that very loud voice of his "Wait till I see that bugger Hume, I'll clock him, I'll stick it where he won't be able to switch it on or off!" With that he strode off back to his desk, much to the amusement of the whole office.

I put the clock into George's drawer out of the way thinking it might go off again although that was hardly likely. George came back into the office about ten minutes to knocking-off time and before I could warn him that Joe MacBride was going to perform a taxidermist operation on his anatomy, Joe spotted him and called him over. Now he's for it, I thought, for Joe had a nasty temper when he was roused. Come five o' clock we all left the office with George still being lectured. It was not until the next morning that I found out that Joe's bark was worse than his bite, for although he told George not to leave alarm clocks on his bench, they had spent the rest of the time chatting about their local pubs with respect to the quality of the beer, for they both liked their pint.

George just laughed when I told him what had happened with the alarm clock. He said he had set the alarm earlier that morning with the intention of checking if the alarm sounded during the lunch period. He was not happy when he saw how we had stopped the ringing with a piece of rag. He said you should have switched it off. I said we would have done if we could have found the lever to do so. George took hold of the clock and pointed to a tiny lever placed underneath the edge of one of the bells. I could not believe it, how anybody would find that lever after just being woken up was beyond comprehension but there again, perhaps that was the idea so you would have to get up straight away or be deafened by the noise of "the bells, the bells!" Perhaps this type of clock should have been named 'The Quasimodo Alarm', it would certainly have given you the 'hump' first thing in the morning, particularly when you found you could not turn it off.

22. The Staff

At this time there were about six apprentices, including myself, working in the electrical drawing office. Namely, Matty Burns, who was the oldest, John Early, who was misnamed, for he was always late for work, Brian Robson (not famous) whose father used to work for my father in the Bass brewery store in Newcastle, Tommy Cole, a lad from Percy Main who was a very good all round sportsman, and last but not least Neville Pointer who was always trying to make extra money over and above his weekly salary by selling all types of items from clothes to electrical goods. Where he got the goods from he wouldn't say. We suspect his wife had a catalogue where they bought various items which Neville would then bring to the office to try to sell.

Brian and I became very good friends throughout our drawing office careers, mainly instigated through our fathers' friendship. Sometimes the apprentices and some of the draughtsmen would go up to the company sports ground and play in an interdepartmental cricket tournament. I was never very keen to participate as I had a nasty experience at school with a cricket ball when I was knocked out attempting to catch very close to the wicket. This put me off cricket as from then on I was afraid of the ball, so I only used to play for the electrical drawing office team when they were short of players

Football, now that was a different ball-game (if you excuse the pun). I loved to play the game and watch it. In my early teens I played for a Boys Brigade church team called St Anthony's who played in the Methodist League where your changing room was the church hall if you were lucky, as some of the teams had no changing facilities. In these circumstances, we would travel to the match wearing our football strip under our ordinary attire. This was alright in fine weather but in the rain and snow our football gear would be soaking wet and muddy so we would have to walk back to the church hall to get washed and changed, which could be half a mile away from the pitch.

Sometimes my hands were so cold I had to get one of the girls to fasten my trouser buttons for me (there were no zips in those days). Mind you I always picked a girl I was going out with at that time but even so it was embarrassing, me being a shy lad. After the game everyone would be invited back to the home team's church hall where we would be given a huge 'chapel tea'. Afterwards, we'd all enjoy a social evening of dancing and games. Those footballing days were some of my happiest experiences as a teenager. I do recall that I was once invited to play for the Northumberland youth team as right back, but that was as far as I got to reaching higher status for we were beaten 2-1 in a cup competition. And anyway, I did not like playing fullback, centre-half was my position. I was only about twenty years old when I had to give up playing football as I damaged my cartilage. It was then I started to take a keen interest in Newcastle United and supported them at St. James's Park for many years and I still take a keen interest in them to this day.

There were eight senior draughtsmen in the office and each was a character in his own right. The oldest was Cecil Fraser who was a section leader and a very good one at that. Cecil was a man who had a vast experience as a draughtsman and shared his knowledge willingly to those who worked in his section. I learnt a great deal from Cecil during the short time I worked for him. Cecil was not a person to socialise, it always appeared to me that he lived only for his work for he never participated in any of the office social events.

Laurie Hettick, referred to as Hank because he was always reading cowboy books, was the artist of the office. Hank was used in the office for his artistic skills rather than his electrical knowledge. If a painting of the shipyard or local area was required for presentation to an owner etc or any special printing or writing required, then Hank was your man. He really was a very good artist.

Hank had a generous nature, willing to do anything for anybody for nothing was a trouble to him. I still have an oil painting that he painted for me depicting Tynemouth Priory and the mouth of the river Tyne looking from the south as it would have been in the eighteenth century.

Hank and I became very good friends and at one time we considered setting up business together. The principal idea was to produce framed pictures of old maps of cities or towns with the main features of that particular town printed on the map with a brief description alongside. The map would also depict any famous or historical monuments. Hank had already produced some maps of the local area and also a picture showing the Roman Wall with all the relative details written alongside specific items depicted on the drawing. These maps sold like hot cakes in our local area of Tyneside and this is where we got the idea of making these maps/drawings of other towns and cities and selling them to the locals. My job would have been to gather interesting information on any town or city and provide transport information while Hank would do the drawings. We both thought about the idea long and hard but in the end decided it was too much of a risk. I think it could have taken off but I had too much to lose, for at that time I was married with a mortgage to be paid, and I had a steady job that I liked. Unfortunately Hank died within ten years of our proposed business adventure, so it would not have left a great deal of time for us to make our fortune.

Joe Barber was a section leader who knew his job well. He was also the gambler of the office as he liked a flutter on the horses and enjoyed a night out at the dogs. Joe also ran the office football pool syndicate to which most of us contributed each week the princely sum of an old shilling. I was in this syndicate for about ten years or more and I cannot recall ever winning anything, although I vividly recall the week I stopped contributing they won, although it could not have been a vast amount as they didn't retire.

Anything to do with gambling Joe would be running it; from the office Derby Day flutter, to a bet on what make of car would park in front of the office entrance on a ship launch day. The winnings were never more than two or three pounds although that was good money in those days. I recall how excited I was when I once won five shillings on one of Joe's gambles. It meant I could take a girl out to the pictures and pay for us both instead of asking her to pay for herself and there would be enough left to buy her an ice cream. I felt like the last of the big spenders.

Joe was also the office union representative and, apart from collecting the union fees every week from the members, he would also attend local, and occasionally national, union meetings. Bill Ryle was a leading draughtsman / section leader, a perfectionist at his work, although to look at him you'd think he was a tramp, for he had little dress sense and he was not particularly attractive to look at. However Bill did have a very good command of the English language and spoke 'the Queen's English' without any dialect, which more than made up for his appearance. Bill had a nasty habit of picking his nose in public without being conscious of doing it and he used to use small pieces of washed out tracing cloth as a handkerchief. I don't think he possessed a proper handkerchief.

You may wonder if Bill had any good qualities. Yes, he was good at his job but there again he was untidy. His drawing bench was always covered with drawings and papers which were not relevant to the task he was performing. I never forgot Bill's philosophy on married life. He said that you should always make a will once you're married for you never know how long you're going to live. He reckoned you should put a clause in your will stating that the wife would only inherit your money providing she made a written signed statement saying she would not marry anyone else after your death. I thought this was strange and a bit unfair on the wife, particularly if she was young, but who was I to question the experience of my elder? When I did query his motive behind the Will statement, he said that he (in his forties) had not worked hard and saved all these years for some Irish navvy to come along after he had gone and reap the benefits of his hard earned money. Pure fantasy I thought, but Bill could not bear the thought of someone else getting their hands on his money and if he could prevent it, then he'd go to his grave a happy man.

George Taylor was an excellent draughtsman, very neat and tidy in all that he did. George, just like Joe, liked to gamble so he and Joe were good friends. George was also a good darts player and used to organise darts games in the lunch hour for those who stayed at work for their lunch. These games used to take place in one corner of the print room where a dartboard would be hung on the wall and a throwing line chalked on the floor.

As well as the ordinary games of darts, there would be competitions and as usual, there was money involved. In these competitions the scorer would stand at one side, quite close to the dartboard so that he could easily see and record the score, while the onlookers stood behind the dart thrower. In one particular game George was scoring and Joe was throwing. Now Joe had a peculiar throwing action. He would release the dart somewhere at about waist height and the dart would invariably hit its target much to the amazement of the rest of us, who normally threw the dart at eye level. Nevertheless, this game Joe threw his first dart which hit the desired target but his second dart went completely off target and stuck in George's hand. George immediately pulled the dart from his hand and clamped his handkerchief over the wound. We found out later when George had returned from the ambulance room that the dart had gone into the back of his hand about a quarter of an inch but had fortunately missed the main artery.

Needless to say the darts scorer never stood anywhere near the dartboard after that. Mind you, Joe had to take some stick from the rest of the lads after the event. They even tried to talk him into changing his throwing style, but to no avail. The funny thing was that when Joe's dart landed in George's hand the rest of us all shouted 'good shot' and burst out laughing, much to the disgust of George who was frantically trying to stop the bleeding.

23. As Fitted

ONE OF THE NICE THINGS about working in the drawing office, apart from the warmth and comfortable surroundings, was that we were still able to visit the yard and go aboard the ships. It was our responsibility not only to produce the working drawings for the tradesmen but also to check that the ship had been fitted out in accordance with those drawings. If any modifications had been made then it was our responsibility to modify the finished drawings accordingly. These were known as 'as fitted' drawings.

Apart from technical discussion about the job, these visits to the yard and ships meant I could keep up-to-date with the news from the many friends I had made while serving my apprenticeship there. As a ship got near to completion there was always a rush to complete the 'as fitted' drawings, hence overtime had to be worked for those who wanted it - a little extra in their pay packets.

If overtime was being worked then you were allowed half an hour to have tea in the canteen which usually comprised sandwiches, cake and as much tea as you wanted. On returning to the office after tea there was always about ten minutes to spare before commencing work, so a few of the draughtsmen and apprentices would kick around between the drawing benches a rolled up piece of tracing cloth held together by brown paper and sticky tape. The idea was to keep this so called ball in the air, passing it between each row of benches, which proved quite a feat considering the amount of space between the benches. Of course there were mishaps where someone would toe–end the underside of the bench, shouting verbal abuse at those of us who found it quite amusing.

The benches sloped from the top to the base at an angle of about twenty degrees which made the task of drawing easier and at the base edge there was a narrow strip of wood running the full length of the bench to prevent drawing instruments and pencils from rolling off. Each draughtsman had an elongated block of wood which prevented the bottles of red and black ink which stood in it from sliding down the bench. I have described this set up purely to enlarge on the picture of one of the footballing events which took place during one over-time shift.

The ball was passed nicely between the drawing benches by skilful footwork and heading when one of the apprentices swung at the ball, missed it and banged his toe right under the edge of the bench. He hit it so hard that the bench vibrated and spilled a bottle of black ink which slowly trickled down over one of the 'as fitted' drawings. After the painful cry of the 'bench kicker' and the laughter of the rest of us, there was a mad scramble by those nearest to retrieve the ink bottle but to no avail as by this time the contents of the bottle were empty and spreading slowly over the drawing. There was no way that the ink could be removed - the drawing was completely ruined. The drawing was quickly confiscated before the management could see it and for the rest of the shift a draughtsman and apprentice had to hastily redraw what had been lost. Mind you it could have been worse -it could have been my drawing!

On the subject of destroyed drawings, there was an even worse calamity one afternoon when Joe Barber was walking up the alleyway towards the print room carrying about three or four 'as fitted' drawings under his arm. As he passed the emergency fire bucket his attention was distracted somehow and the drawings slid from his arm straight into the bucket of water, totally destroying them.

This was no laughing matter as the drawings were required for the ship which was leaving the yard at the weekend although there were a few of us who saw the funny side of the event. Needless to say it was all hands to the drawing board to redraw that which was lost. We achieved the deadline with time to spare. The fire bucket was given a wire mesh cap to prevent any further mishaps.

24. The Christmas Party

THROUGHOUT THE YEAR Joe used to collect a shilling a week from those who wanted to participate in the annual Christmas party. This event was for electrical draughtsmen only plus special invited guests. The event took place the last afternoon before the company shut down for the Christmas and New Year break.

The venue was a drying room situated in one corner of the large print room which led off from the electrical drawing office. The drying room was about thirty feet long by fifteen feet wide and was used for drying special developed blue prints and linen prints produced by Ned Costigan, the printer. Ned was a lovely natured chap to whom nothing was a trouble, a nice old man. I say old because anyone over thirty in those days was old to me; I guess Ned would be in his late fifties. Anyway, a week before the event, invitations were sent to a dozen of the best looking girls in the wages department to attend the party which would start at four thirty.

On the day of the party, a number of us, with the permission of Joe McBride our deputy boss, would clean the drying room, erect a portable bar at one end, arrange seating around the rest of the room and furnish it with Christmas decorations. Coloured lights were fitted giving the effect of a dimly lit Aladdin's cave. It really was an unbelievable transformation. While the decoration was going on Joe and George would be arranging to collect all the booze which was a considerable amount from a year's weekly subscription paid by each member of staff.

There would be every conceivable type of spirit, cocktails, beer and soft drinks to help make the party go with a swing. I should point out that I was teetotal at this time. There was a buffet laid on which I understand was purchased from the canteen and in addition one of the draughtsmen used to provide a large Christmas cake baked by his mother. The party did not really get going until the girls arrived. Once the alcohol had taken effect, it was time for a dance and sing-along to the strains of Pat Boone and other popular singers of that era from a portable 78rpm. Gramophone loaned by one of the apprentices.

Joe, Ned Costigan and I enjoyed singing and we made a very pleasant sound as a trio, so when there was a lull in the proceedings, the three of us would strike up a lively melody, although our favourite songs were usually of the weepy type which also went down well. Joe and Ned could never understand how I could enjoy myself so much on only soft drinks. The girls, or I should say ladies as most of them were quite a bit older than me, made the party go with a swing joining in the fun, even to the extent of a number of them having snogging sessions with some of the lads.

I recall there was a particularly attractive looking blonde there called Sybil who caught my eye, who at that point in time was being given mouth to mouth resuscitation by Joe. Now I am very partial to blondes and always have been, so I was not going to miss out sampling the best looking girl in the room even though she was about five years older than me. My opportunity came when Joe was called to the bar to refill someone's glass as he was acting barman. I don't recall the details of my approach or patter but I do remember her kiss. It was like having a rubber sink plunger placed over my mouth creating a vacuum so great that after awhile I could not breathe and eventually had to tear myself away from her before I fainted. Not the pleasant experience I expected. Enough of these intimate details.

The party went on until about eight thirty with half of those attending mildly drunk and the rest of us feeling happy in the knowledge of having enjoyed another well organised electrical drawing office Christmas party.

25. Maturing and Moving On

ACROSS THE OTHER SIDE of the building directly opposite to our drawing office was the ship's drawing office, the largest office in the building. This was where all the main ship drawings were produced and was controlled by a chief draughtsman named Jimmy Brown, although every one addressed him as Mr. Brown. Mr. Brown was a very stern and dour Scotsman who never smiled and seldom had a kind word for anyone but knew how to get work out of people. I was walking past his office whistling some tune or other, for I had a habit of whistling wherever I went and still do to this day. He suddenly bellowed out behind me in a raw Scottish twang, "Storp that blady whistlin laddie. If ye had been meant ti whistle ye would have had wings". I don't know why but Mr. Brown could not stand whistling and would not tolerate it in his office. He was a first class draughtsman who knew almost everything about ship design which I suppose was why he was chief draughtsman.

Life as a draughtsman was quite pleasant and the money was reasonable, allowing me to contribute a fair sum to my mother towards the rent and upkeep of the house. The only thing to spoil it was the uncertainty of when I would have to commence my eighteen months National service. I was now twenty one and unless I was working on naval vessels for the Ministry of Defence I could not be deferred. However Mr Birbeck, our chief draughtsman, told me that he intended to defer my conscription into one of the armed services as long as possible.

On the subject of conscription, one of my colleagues was working on the lighting drawings of a passenger liner when he was called to do his National service. Now once you had completed your service, the company was obliged to take you back into their employment. My colleague duly returned after eighteen months, reported to the chief draughtsman and asked him what work he should do. The Chief replied "Oh, just carry on with the lighting drawings where you left off", much to his surprise.

In that eighteen months he had been away nothing had progressed on the work he had been doing and it made no difference to the completion programme of the ship for the design and build period for a liner in those days would be about four to five years. Hence there was always a reasonable length of time to do your job and do it neatly and correctly, unlike today when everything is wanted yesterday, although in those days we did not have computers to speed up the work process. Every year the company held a staff dinner dance at one of Newcastle's more elegant venues, namely the Old Assembly Rooms in the centre of town.

Invitations were restricted to staff members and their wives or partners. Dress was formal evening wear. Tickets for the event were generously subsidised by the company. Being just a young lad with little money, I could not afford my own evening suit so had to hire one from the famous Dormies hire company.

My girlfriend at that time and for many more staff dances in the future, was a blonde called Joan Lillie, the tastiest dish in St. Anthony's since mince & dumplings. Joan was a very slim and attractive blonde. She was quite shy, just like myself which meant we both got on well together. We also shared the same interests, namely church youth club, dancing and tennis. We both loved dancing and regularly participated not only at church socials but also at the local dance halls. Along with dancing, tennis was our favourite sport. We both enjoyed the privilege of being Captain and Vice Captain of the church tennis club and we both played in competitive matches for the club team.

The staff dance was the social occasion of the year. Everything about the occasion was exciting for both Joan and me. Being smartly dressed, a taxi would take us to the event where we would meet colleagues, enjoy what was always a delicious five course meal, then listen to the company speech, usually given by the Chairman, telling us how well the company had progressed over the last year but always insisting we need to do better. Then, with dinner over, we would all ascend the grand winding staircase leading into the ballroom where we would enjoy the rest of the evening dancing to the Josh Q. Atkinson Orchestra and chatting and drinking with our friends before partaking of light supper refreshments at around midnight. Dancing would consist at that time of modern waltz, quick step, foxtrot, tango, plus all the popular old fashioned dances. The dance would end at about one o' clock the following morning when we'd all depart for home in a happy state of mind having enjoyed ourselves, not forgetting the added bonus of occasionally winning a raffle or spot prize.

In 1953, my career had reached a stage where I could no longer evade National service. I didn't relish the idea of going into one of the services for two years although I had decided long before that when I did have to go then my preference would be the Royal Navy. However that choice never materialised, for I discovered that if I joined the Merchant Navy and served more than two years with them then that would count as my National service. The only difference being that the shipyard would be obliged to reinstate me as a draughtsman after National service, whereas if I went into the Royal Navy, I would have to leave the company with no guarantee of employment when I returned. The major factor that convinced me to go into the Merchant Navy was that I would be able to continue in my chosen profession of electrical engineering. Only instead of contributing towards the building of ships, I would now be able to further my experience in the practical side of operating and servicing ships electrically.

My next step was to apply to the various merchant shipping companies for a position. Of the many replies I received, the one that appealed to me was an offer to join the Peninsular and Oriental Steam Navigation Company (P. & O.) as a supernumerary electrical engineering officer. After a favourable interview in London, P. & O. offered me the position and instructed me to report back to their offices in Leadenhall Street in three weeks. This enabled me to terminate my employment with Vickers shipyard and sort out what was required in my new job.

I was very nervous and apprehensive as I travelled down to London bearing in mind that I was starting a new career with new colleagues and my first job away from home.

My first assignment was to report to Tilbury Docks and join a 27,955 ton passenger liner named 'Himalaya' which had just returned from Australia and was due to return there after two weeks in Tilbury. Whist at Tilbury, the ship had to be replenished with supplies of food, drink, etc. as well as repairs being carried out where necessary. Half the crew would go on leave the first week in port and the other half the second week. Those of us who weren't sailing with the ship were assigned to what was called dock staff duties which comprised mainly light repairs and servicing of equipment. Dock Staff also comprised pursers and navigation officers who in turn would be carrying out their specific duties during the ship's two-week turnaround.

All dock staff lived and took meals on board the ship and when that ship left, moved onto the next one that arrived and so on until there was a vacant post on board that required filling. It should be pointed out that P. & O. had about ten liners in service operating from Tilbury Docks and about twenty two cargo ships most of which operated from the King George the Fifth Docks further up the River Thames. Being on dock staff enabled me to get kitted out with the various uniforms I would require once I got posted to a ship. There was the best 'Barathea' fine wool cloth uniform with cap, black tie, socks and shoes and white shirts to buy. There were also two tropical uniforms and dinner jackets, white socks and shoes, black bow tie and cummerbund as well as white boiler suits to work in. This kit, as you can imagine, was quite expensive and I certainly couldn't afford to purchase it there and then. Fortunately P. & O. had an arrangement with the outfitters, Miller Raynor & Haysom in Tilbury, to provide their crew with the uniforms, etc. required and the cost paid for by P. & O. who in turn deducted so much per month off your salary. The only thing I had to pay for up front was a set of tools and electrical instruction manuals.

26. Officer and Gentleman

I was on dock staff working on various liners from about October to December 1953, when I was finally assigned to my first ship. This by some phenomenal coincidence happened to be the S.S. Strathmore, the very first ship I had served part of my apprenticeship on back at Vickers naval yard. The ship derived its name from the late Queen Mother's father, the Earl of Strathmore. She was a 23,428 ton passenger liner built by Vickers Armstrongs shipyard at Barrow-in-Furness in 1935. Her engines comprised six single reduction geared steam turbines. She was propelled by two screws which attained a cruising speed of 20 knots. The total crew complement was 503 and she could accommodate 445 first class and 665 tourist class passengers. The ship carried five electrical officers, the chief, the second, the third and two supernumeraries one of which was me.

The second coincidence in joining my first ship was that the chief electrical officer was a Geordie named Eddie Davison from Percy Main, a little village further down the Tyne to Walker where I lived. What a good start, a Geordie boss and a familiar ship and the experience of having worked in a shipyard: things looked promising.

My accommodation was a small cabin no more than nine feet (3 metres) by seven and a half feet (2 metres). It contained a single bed, a wardrobe, a set of drawers, a tiny writing table, a miniature armchair and a sink with a porthole above it looking out onto the tourist class passenger deck. It was one of the smallest officer's cabins on the ship and the least private, for curious passengers would often peer through the porthole. This meant I had to draw my curtain for privacy so blocking out the natural light.

The cabin was particularly uncomfortable in the tropics when I would have the porthole open to let in fresh air, for we only had a forced air system to ventilate the cabin as there was no air conditioning. In the tropics the temperatures could get above the eighties in the cabin at night with the vents blowing in warm air which made it difficult to sleep. Still, I survived.

On one occasion I was getting changed and was standing putting my underpants on when a squeaky voice said "you should draw your curtains, young man", yes I had forgotten about the porthole. After the shock, I quickly went to the porthole to see a little old lady walking away, shoulders shaking. Whether she was laughing or she'd had a fright I'll never know but I made sure after that incident the curtain remained closed when changing.

The Strathmore's principal role was to carry passengers out to Australia and to deliver Royal Mail and cargo to the different countries en-route. Having the contract to carry mail meant that the ship had a strict sailing schedule to observe on the voyage out to Australia and back, which took twelve weeks.

Cargo was carried in her two holds, one positioned forward and one aft. Outgoing to Australia the cargo would invariably be cars and machinery and homeward bound mainly tea, rubber and fruit. The ship was split into two classes, First and Tourist. First Class generally comprised of military or naval personnel returning to their postings and /or passengers on holiday and business trips. Tourist Class had holiday makers and business passengers also, but the majority were emigrant families going out to Australia to seek their fortune, for this was the period when you could emigrate under a government scheme for a bargain price of ten pounds per person.

The ship's staff consisted of deck officers, engineering officers, pursers and general crew. The cabin and restaurant crew were Goanese. The deck crew comprised of Pakistanis. The Engine room crew were Hindustanis. The majority of these different nationalities could speak English but not all; hence we had to learn to converse in their language at times. If you fancied a hot curry then these were the boys to see. Sometimes while repairing equipment in their private galley they would invite me to partake of their curry dish of the day. The first time I accepted their offer I eagerly took a large spoonful which nearly blew my head off. Now I like spicy foods but I have never tasted anything so hot as a Hindustani curry. What their stomachs were like after eating these curries regularly only they would know and I wouldn't like to be anywhere near them once they had digested it!

I found the majority of Goanese, Pakistanis and Hindustanis friendly people who would always be willing to sit and chat about their homeland and families. They were also keen bargain hunters always on the lookout for old second hand sewing machines and bicycles. They would tie the bicycles and sewing machines up in between the deckhead beams of their quarters until they reached Bombay (Mumbai) where they would either take them home or sell them at a lucrative profit, for bicycles and sewing machines were in great demand in India at that time.

The Goanese cabin boys (as we officers called them) liked neat gin so that if you had a bottle in your cabin they would be prone to take a sip. Most officers used to mark the bottle to keep a check on whether the boy had been helping himself.

At Christmas time all officers would be invited to the Goanese quarters where they would be given a triple measure of neat gin to drink. Being teetotal at that time, I had great difficulty in downing the neat gin but had to for it would have been an insult to them not to. I always felt a little light headed after those annual visits.

The ship sailed out of the Thames and into the North Sea on 23rd December, 1953. We passed through the Straits of Dover into the English Channel during the night when the weather started to change, the wind began to blow hard and the sea got quite choppy but the worst was to come. Once we passed Ushant, a small island off the northwest coast of France and sailed into the Bay of Biscay we headed straight into a force eight south westerly gale on Christmas Day.

The ship had a set of stabilisers fitted which were ineffective in the weather we were experiencing. The waves were making the ship pitch and roll at frightening angles and it was unsafe to proceed out onto the open deck as the wind was so fierce.

The first part of my working day began at 7am when I had to check that the ventilation fans were operating satisfactorily in the Tourist area of the ship. I left my cabin feeling a little queasy trying not to think about the excessive movement of the ship but to no avail. I had to admit, I had succumbed to what I had dreaded, sea sickness. I made a dash to the nearest toilet where, unknown to me, the floor had just been washed and was still wet. Two steps inside the toilet my feet slid away from me and I finished up crashing into one of the open toilet doors, ending up sliding on my bottom up against the toilet pan. This was very convenient for all I had to do was lift the seat and bring up every thing I had devoured the day before.

I left the toilet unaware that I had escaped serious injury for I felt so ill. I went to the nearest fan room, flopped on the floor hoping I might recover enough to continue my duties. Five minutes hadn't passed when I was off again running to the toilet, only this time, in a sure footed manner. I didn't think there was anything left inside me to come up but I must have eaten well the previous day.

By this time It was 8am, time for breakfast although that was the last thing on my mind, all I wanted was my bunk. I had no sooner got into my cabin when the chief arrived and on hearing of my escapade the previous hour, he began to insist that I should get something in my stomach which would make me feel better. Being new to the ship I thought I'd better do as I was told, but as the officers dined in the passenger's dining room, it meant I had to shower, shave, shampoo and dress in my uniform.

I duly got down to the dining room, sat down at the engineering officers table and decided to have a dry bread bun as a starter. I had managed to get half the bun down when one of the waiters brought a huge plate of bacon, eggs and sausage for one of my colleagues. I can't remember leaving the dining room, but quickly found a toilet. So much for getting dressed up and going to the dining room for breakfast, I just knew I wouldn't be able to keep anything down.

At 9.15am I had to report to the chief for my work instructions. As it was Christmas Day he said we wouldn't be doing much unless there was an emergency, so I and the other supernumerary were given the task of wiring the Christmas tree in the First Class passengers lounge. My colleague, Peter Kearney came from the Isle of Wight, had studied electrical engineering but hadn't a clue about ships and this was the first time he had set foot on one.

In normal circumstances it wouldn't take two to wire a Christmas tree but we were both feeling seasick. Peter would start to arrange the lights on the tree, then the next minute I would see him disappearing out of the door and leaning over the side of the ship. Then when he returned, I would be off to do the same. One problem was that the wind was blowing towards the side of the ship we were leaning over so you tended to get back what you thought you'd got rid of!

My first lesson, if you are going to be sick over the side, make sure it's the leeward and not the windward side.

We did eventually wire the tree although it took us all morning. This had to be a record. The chief gave us the rest of the day off which pleased us, for I'm sure we weren't capable of working in the state we were in. I immediately retired to my cabin and lay on my bunk feeling really sorry for myself thinking, "Why did I have to come to sea and endure this when I could be at home enjoying a nice Christmas meal and opening presents with the family?" Being seasick is bad enough without also feeling homesick.

Boxing Day followed a similar pattern to the previous day except that we had to work up to 5pm. Peter and I were still feeling very rough for we were still feeling seasick. It was not until the ship had sailed out of the Atlantic Ocean into the Mediterranean Sea that the sea became calmer much to the relief of me and the majority of passengers who hadn't been seen since we left Tilbury Docks.

I found out later from the bosun that the storm we had passed through in the Bay of Biscay was the worst weather he had experienced in the forty years he had been at sea. He also told me that the bay was noted for bad weather at the best of times but for him the last two days must have been a record for roughness. Now that life was back to normal I could get on with the job I was expected to do and enjoy the new experiences of sea life.

The electrical officers were the only personnel in the engineering department that didn't have to work watches which were four hours on and eight hours off. We worked day shifts which comprised 7am to 8am and 9.15am to 12 noon, then 2 to 4pm. Time was then our own until the following morning with the exception of one day in every five when we were on watch duty. The difference here was that after we had done our normal day's work, we had to stay in our cabin on standby duty in case we were called out to do repairs or answer an emergency alarm call during the night. Life didn't seem too bad once you got out of the seasick zone.

One of the tasks of an electrical officer was to show films to both First and Tourist Class passengers. In those days the ship did not have its own cinema. Films were projected from two portable projectors both of which had to be assembled out on the covered outside deck through the starboard First Class lounge window onto a screen on the port side of the lounge. In Tourist Class the projector was set up at one end of a covered outside deck just outside my cabin, onto a screen at the opposite end. The projectors were of the old fashioned 35mm size which meant that a normal film show would have about five reels of film. Once reel one was being shown, you would then load reel two into the other projector ready to change over when reel one was finished. The method of change over was by a flap in front of the lens of each machine which were interconnected so that when one reel of film was finished you opened the other machine's flap which mechanically closed the other flap. On nearing the end of a reel you had to be alert in watching for a black dot appearing in the top right hand corner of the screen which was a signal to start the second projector motor. Then, a second dot which was the signal to change over to the other projector.

You can imagine if you did not get this operation right then you had either cut part of the film off or numbers appeared on the screen much to the disgust of the audience. My first voyage was a disaster as far as film showing was concerned, although not necessarily all my fault.

During a First Class film show, I suddenly noticed that right in the centre of the picture on the screen, a small brown hole appeared which began to enlarge as the film continued until all of a sudden there was a loud explosion. The screen went blank and smoke was pouring out of the projector, amidst booing and slow hand clapping from the audience. The projector motor had stopped so the film heated up and burnt a hole in the centre of the film due to the heat of the internal projection lamp. The film would only burn for a few seconds before a built in gas bottle released an extinguishing gas to prevent a major fire. It did not take me long to remedy the problem, accompanied by much applause from the audience.

Children's film shows were given in the afternoon around four o' clock. They consisted of cartoons which they all loved and clapped and shouted at with pleasure. The projectionist was also a keen fan of these cartoons. One afternoon the lounge was packed with kids and some of the parents of the younger ones. This afternoon there was a slight swell on the sea but nothing to worry about as long as I kept the projectors steady bearing in mind that the films were projected from starboard to port.

The show got underway and the kids were all happily enjoying it when the swell seemed to increase which meant the ship began to roll from port to starboard. At first I managed to hold the projector steady then the machine would move so much that the picture moved off the screen. There I was struggling to keep the picture on the screen with about seventy kids waving and cheering every time the picture moved off the screen. Then disaster struck, a larger swell knocked me off balance prevented me holding the projector and over it went onto the deck.

Meanwhile there was pandemonium in the lounge with kids thrown off their seats crying and shouting for their parents, it was absolute bedlam. I managed to muster a few stewards and we set about restoring some form of order in the lounge. Fortunately no one was seriously hurt, only a few scratches and bumps.

One of the most amusing episodes of my career as a projectionist took place one evening in the Tourist section where I was about to show a mystery film. I had commenced the show and got to the third reel of film when I realised I had shown the third reel before the second reel. So after seeing the first reel of film they then saw the third reel followed by the second reel of film. All was quiet in the audience each one of them apparently intrigued by this mystery film. I then continued with the film reels in the correct order. After the film show, people came up to me and thanked me for giving the show, saying how much they had enjoyed it. There was one or two who commented on the fact that it was hard to follow in parts. No-one had twigged that I had got the reels mixed up, little did they know!

Sometimes showing films became boring, particularly when you had shown it two or three times on a voyage. One trip I showed The Dambusters film eight times, I knew the film off by heart. I could tell you exactly when the bombs would be dropped and when they would explode and how many casualties there would be. During this boredom, I would read a book and become so engrossed in it, I'd forget to change the reels over and would only realise by the shouting of the audience. You think a projectionist's job is easy, it wasn't in those days.

P. & O. were very strict on dress on board their vessels which meant that if you were working out on deck or in any of the Public Rooms where passengers were going to be, then clean white overalls had to be worn. If you were off duty then you had to wear full winter or tropical uniform. This depended on what the Captain deemed as 'dress of the day' which was usually governed by the outside temperature. If you were going to the dining saloon for your meals then full uniform was worn except for dinner, when mess kits and bow tie would be worn. This was something unique about P. & O., in the fact that they were the only company that allowed all of their officers to dine in the passengers' dining saloon.

Senior officers each hosted a passenger table and the rest of the officers dined at their own table, the engineering staff on the port side just inside the entrance into the saloon and the navigating and pursers staff on the starboard side. This meant if you sat at the forward end of the table you could survey all the passengers dining. In fact you could still see the passengers even if you sat on the other side of the table, for there was a large mirror covering the whole of the port side bulkhead.

One of the main perks was that we dined from the passenger menu. Apart from being able to use the passenger sports deck in our leisure time, in the evenings we were allowed the use of one passenger public rooms. This was the dance floor area where we could take coffee after dinner and participate in the social events which were scheduled for that evening. This could be anything from dancing to horse racing to bingo.

With these privileges, life as an officer on a P. & O. liner wasn't too bad at all.

27. Port Said to Aden

THE SHIP'S FIRST PORT OF CALL was Port Said in Egypt. It is the northern entrance to the Suez Canal and the gateway to Cairo and the pyramids. It was here that we took on fresh water and oil. As soon as the ship was tied up alongside, seemingly from nowhere would come the 'bum boats' full of souvenirs ready for the passengers to buy.

It was interesting and laughable at times to hear the bargaining that took place between the crafty Egyptian sellers and the gullible passengers. It wasn't until a few trips later that I made my first purchase from one of the 'bum boats' as I was then more aware of the true value of the wares they were selling. My purchase was a carved wooden camel stool with a leather cushion and an all leather pouffe, a bargain at three pounds plus two fresh bread rolls from the engineers' mess. I wonder just how many thousands of P.& O. passengers and crew have had these two Egyptian pieces of furniture gracing their homes over the years.

Those officers and crew who were not on duty were allowed to go ashore but were warned to stay in groups of at least four people and not to get into any trouble. Apparently it was unsafe to walk some of the streets on your own. On hearing this warning I declined to go ashore and have to admit, never have had any desire to do so in all the visits I paid to that port.

After leaving Port Said with our Egyptian pilot on board we began our passage through the Suez Canal. This is a sea level waterway running north and south connecting the Mediterranean and Red Sea and separating the African continent from Asia. The canal is 105 miles (168 km) from Port Said on the Mediterranean to Suez in the Red Sea, utilising three intervening lakes namely, Lake Menzala, Lake Timseh and the Bitter Lakes. The canal only permits single line traffic, one way at a time. It was in the Bitter Lakes that the southbound vessels anchored whilst the northbound vessels passed on their journey to Port Said. Once all the northbound traffic was through, then the southbound continued their journey south through the rest of the canal.

The Canal was designed by a Frenchman named Ferdinand De Lessops and was completed in 1869 and provided the shortest maritime route between Europe and the Indian and Western Pacific Oceans. To the west of the canal is the low lying delta of the Nile and to the east is the higher rugged and arid Sinai peninsular. The total journey time from Port Said to the Gulf of Suez was eleven and a half hours. My first journey through the canal was an exciting experience. The canal channel was quite narrow with little room to spare on either side of the vessel as she moved forward at a slow rate of knots. It was weird to see desert on both sides as the ship sailed through this deep channel. On the port side of the canal there was a major dusty road running parallel all the way to Suez. During our passage south I noticed teams of workmen laying huge stone slabs along the base of the canal, just exactly what they were doing wasn't apparent. What really interested me was the fact that each stone slab was being carried on an arab's head and supported by the arms of each workman, part of a long line of them, transporting the stones from the top of the canal bank down to the bottom. It was a scene from the past, no cranes or lorries to be seen.

During our passage through the canal during the day, the passengers would be entertained by the Egyptian magician known as the 'Gully Gully' man who would board the ship in Port Said. Why he was named the 'Gully Gully' man I have never been able to find out, perhaps it was that his audience was gullible to the various aspects of his act. I recall he had this uncanny feat of producing a vast number of hens eggs from seemingly nowhere, much to the delight of his audience.

During the darkness of night it was part of my job to operate the ship's searchlight. This was fitted inside a small compartment fitted at the bow of the ship where the P. & O. crest was fitted. This crest could be opened upwards to enable the searchlight to be positioned as far forward thus enabling the beam of the light to illuminate the canal and bank side ahead of the ship. Once the light was operating there wasn't much to do but sit in a deck chair and wait until the burning carbon rods which produced the light needed renewing. This duty was considered a perk, for apart from having the following morning off, you were given a bottle of rum. The idea was that it was so cold in the searchlight compartment that the rum was to help warm you up, but the rum was never issued to you until the following morning as it was felt that you may end up drunk before the night was over . Anyway I always got well wrapped up for this duty and it would have made little difference having the bottle at that time, for as I said, I was teetotal. My bottle was shared out amongst my colleagues, although later on in my sea career I acquired a taste for rum and ginger beer. It was from this concoction that I experienced what it was like to be drunk.

One lunch time sitting in my cabin with my close colleagues sharing my rum and ginger beer, I had to nip out to the toilet. I should mention that each of us had a pint glass of which a third of it was filled with rum and the rest ginger beer. On my return, I hadn't noticed that someone had topped my glass up with more rum, as my glass emptied, I decided that it was time for me to eat. As I was on watch duty that day I was allowed to eat in the engineers' mess which was only about fifteen yards from my cabin. I can't remember how I got there but I do recall sitting at the lunch table talking to the chief refrigerating engineer whilst eating my lunch. Come the time to return to my cabin, I recall staggering up the alleyway bouncing off each bulkhead wondering what was happening to me. It was about five thirty in the afternoon when I eventually woke to find that I had slept for four and a half hours through the afternoon. Later the fridge engineer whom I had dined with in the mess came to see how I was and told me that throughout the meal I had continuously talked a load of garble to him. That was and has been the only time that I have ever experienced being drunk.

Continuing on with my first voyage after passing through the Suez Canal, the ship then entered the Red Sea where the temperature soared into the nineties. The hot weather brought the passengers out on deck to sunbathe. This was a signal for the officers to eye-up the young talent available, but more about that later.

As we sailed in excessively warm conditions down through the Red Sea passing Saudi Arabia on the port side and Egypt then Sudan on the starboard side, one was made aware of the vast unpopulated areas of these countries. Also the clear blue sea all around us with so many species of brightly coloured fish swimming alongside the ship and with a clear blue sky above. This setting had to be one of the highlights of the passage. In all the places I've visited throughout the world I cannot recall seeing such beautiful sunrises and sunsets as I witnessed in the Red Sea. One can't give it justice in trying to describe the continuous changing colour that was prevalent on those occasions.

Our next port of call was Aden, at the southern end of Yemen. It was a small town with just one main street which consisted mainly of shops although at one end of the town there was a small park. Aden was the cheapest place in the world in the 1950's for duty free gifts. You could purchase anything from rings and watches to shoes and clothes.

All passengers went ashore here to buy their presents. It was also a favourite with the crew for buying their wife or girlfriend a present. The most popular present bought by the crew was a box with seven pairs of ladies' brief frilly panties in it. Each pair a different colour, with each day of the week printed on them. I was never brave enough to buy a set, not that I could think of any girl I'd give them to.

The main reason for stopping at Aden was to take on fresh water again, as we didn't have our own fresh water distilling units. Aden fresh water was the foulest water that I have ever tasted. It had a taste of its own which tended to make you feel sick. The problem was that the water tanks never emptied of this foul stuff until we reached Australia. The only decent way to drink it was to mix it with orange juice or, for the hardened drinker, gin or whisky.

I was allowed to go ashore in Aden, as indeed in most ports (seeing as it was my first trip) which I thought was very generous of the chief. I had strolled along the main street looking in most of the shops and buying an odd souvenir here and there, when I decided to go and sit in the park to try and cool off, for the temperature here was well into the nineties. I hadn't been sat there for long when the heavens opened and it started to absolutely pour with rain. A mad dash across the road to the shops got me safely under cover and while standing there I noticed all the locals and shopkeepers running outside and standing in the rain with their arms raised enjoying every minute of the downpour. This puzzled me at first until I found out from one shopkeeper that it had not rained in Aden for two and a half years.

This was becoming a first trip of records what with the roughest Bay of Biscay crossing in forty years and now rain in Aden after two and a half years. What next?

It was in Aden on a later trip that a colleague and I decided to explore further inland to see what the countryside was like. We hired a taxi and set off towards the town of Ta'izz which nestled at the foot of the mountains. On the way there we passed through a range of small hills with what appeared to be lots of caves, the entrance to which were covered with cardboard boxes. Our driver informed us that some of the poorer people lived in these caves and cardboard boxes.

The whole of the terrain around us as we travelled was barren of any greenery what so ever, even the road was just a stony, dusty track, which made the ride pretty uncomfortable. I cannot remember ever seeing a country so bleak. My colleague, David, and I decided we had seen enough and asked the driver to return to our ship.

Another occasion we decided to climb up one of the adjacent hills overlooking the port to get a better view of the harbour and its surroundings and take photographs. We had almost reached the top when there was a loud report of a gun being fired. We looked around but could not see anyone until

David spotted on the adjacent hillside what appeared to be two soldiers with rifles slung over their shoulders. They were obviously out on patrol looking for someone and whether they had fired their guns we weren't sure but both David and I decided not to wait and find out. We went down that hill at breakneck speed until we reached the bottom, before daring to look up to see where the soldiers were or if they were coming after us. We realised it was a stupid venture in a strange land with a different culture, of which we knew nothing. We never had time to witness the view or take photographs!

28. Aden to Colombo

W<small>E LEFT ADEN</small> after our short, five hour stay and headed out into the Arabian Sea for the Port of Bombay (now renamed Mumbai on the west coast of India. It was a fairly smooth crossing for a change. This sea was not always conducive to a smooth crossing, particularly in the monsoon period when the sea could be quite rough. With incessant rain and very high temperatures it was most uncomfortable, to put it mildly.

It was during this passage that I learned a couple of lessons about women. By this time I had been introduced to all the staff which included female nurses, nursery nurses and stenographers. One evening one of the nursery nurses, who was in her early forties, much older than me, invited me into her cabin, the reason for which I fail to remember. After accepting a soft drink, much to her disgust that I wouldn't take anything stronger, we chatted for the next hour or so. As time passed, she was getting a lot more talkative with her consumption of gin and tonic and starting to move a little closer to me which suddenly set warning bells off for me. It wasn't as though she was attractive, she was hard looking and well past her 'sell by' date and anyway, I wasn't interested.

Every time I moved away she moved closer so I decided it was time to go and immediately made some excuse and left quickly, much to her disgust. One of the engineers who had been on the ship for over a year on hearing of my evening's escapade, told me that this was a regular event with her with all new officers for she was desperate to have a man. He said that she was known amongst the staff as 'the Old Boot', which applied to any girl over the age of forty. She certainly looked well worn and down at heel.

Then there was one evening about nine o' clock when I was on watch duty, I got a call from one of the passenger cabins to say that their bed light wasn't working. Off I went with my tool kit ready to do a quick repair job or hopefully just replace a burnt out lamp. On reaching the cabin, I knocked and waited until a female voice shouted, "Come in!" On entering I saw a very attractive young female lying on top of her bed dressed in what could only be described as a flimsy night gown that was revealing more than it should. My first reaction was to leave immediately, for P.& O. had a strict rule that anyone caught fraternising in a passenger's cabin would be instantly dismissed. Then I thought, if there was something wrong with the light and I ignored it, she could still get me into trouble. I finished up asking her to switch the light on which she did and it illuminated immediately whereby she smiled and patted the bed cover. This was my cue to beat a hasty retreat, for no way was I going to break company rules, particularly on my first voyage. Pity about those rules, for she was an attractive looking lady! Two lessons I learnt, avoid 'Old Boots' and passenger temptresses.

I felt quite excited when at last we arrived in India in the early hours of the morning. The first thing you notice as you enter the port of Bombay is this magnificent decorated building surrounding a huge archway which is known as 'The Gateway to India'. As soon as we had tied up alongside the quay, from nowhere would appear hordes of beggars and taxi-rickshaws waiting to pounce on the passengers as they went ashore.

Once again Peter and I ware allowed to go ashore, so we went together. The Port itself was the filthiest I had witnessed on my travels and the smell was obnoxious. It was difficult to walk around Bombay without being accosted by beggars. You really had to try and ignore them for if you gave to one there would be another twenty or more pestering you. It was really pitiful to see young children with limbs missing. I was told the limb was removed just after birth so that it would be easier to make a living begging later in life. How the parents got away with this I'll never know but it certainly did take place. The thinking behind this was that the child would stand a better chance of surviving by playing on the sympathy and generosity of those donating money who were sorely moved at their plight. There seemed to me to be too many deformed children and adults in Bombay for there not to be some truth in this rumour.

During the day, the city of Bombay was a mass of people and traffic all of which appeared to be in a frantic hurry and cocooned in a continuous din of blasting motor horns. Most of the traffic seemed to comprise old single deck buses, old lorries stacked high with goods of all description, British Morris Oxford cars as taxis, rickshaws and bicycles conveying people and goods - all skilfully weaving their way in and out of this continuous bustle. It was also a colourful scene with the different patterns of the women's saris and even some of the men's dhotis (loin cloths) and shirts.

Crossing one of the bridges overlooking a stretch of water in the city, there was the local 'wash centre' (known in India as a Dhobi Ghat) close to the water's edge. It was laid out in the form of open cubicles made out of stone where the Indian women went to wash their clothes. Each woman or family of females would occupy a cubicle, soak their washing in water, and then begin to beat it on the stone floor of the cubicle to get it clean. I never saw any soap being used but assumed they must have had at least a bar of carbolic to get the dirt out of the clothes. This was only one of the many primitive actions I saw still used in this part of the world.

Peter and I soon left the main roads and took to exploring some of the back-streets of the city. Here we found rows of flats on either side with a few shops, also young children playing and laughing together while their mothers and older members of the family looked on. Our appearance immediately aroused interest and for a moment I was beginning to regret that we had decided to venture away from the main thoroughfare. Having given the kids that were there a few 'annas' each, we decided to proceed in the knowledge that the crowd that had now gathered to see us were really only curious to see two tall Englishmen dressed all in white i.e. white shirt, shorts, long white socks and white shoes. This was a P. & O. officer's dress when going ashore unless he decided to wear civvies but these were usually too warm. I was aware that there was a lot of whispering and giggling going on at our expense but I really didn't mind for I was quite enjoying being the centre of attention even though it may have been for the wrong reason. The families were large and looked very poor, and most parents had their grandparents living with them. Indian grandparents were respected by their children who would automatically look after them in their later years, a custom to be admired and which I believe is still carried out today, not only there, but by Indians living here in Britain.

Moving along the street Peter and I got our first glimpse of one of the noted Indian sacred cows - a very thin and bony looking animal which enjoyed the rare privilege of being able to wander where it liked throughout the city and enjoying the scraps of food discarded by the locals. It was when we were observing the cow that a taxi came along and had to stop as the cow stood in the middle of the road. One would have expected a blast on the car horn but no, the taxi driver waited patiently until the cow was ready to move to one side and enable him to pass. Nothing takes preference over the sacred cow. I was only too pleased that I wasn't a paying passenger in the taxi!

A little further on we passed a woman sat on the kerb-side with her skirt pulled up above her knees which were spread apart in a most undignified position. As we passed her on the other side of the road she shouted after us in Indian but we just kept walking. It wasn't until later that we found out that she was one of the local prostitutes begging for custom. She could have begged all day as far as Peter and I were concerned for she must have been at least fifty or more in years and looked absolutely filthy.

One thing I couldn't stand was the smells. What with the cow dung drying in temperatures well into the nineties and all the different sickly perfumes from both men and women as they passed by, the combination made me feel ill. Also the disgusting habit of some of the men who would be chewing beetle nut, which was a small red nut which when chewed produced a red saliva which they would habitually spit out on to the pavement.

In India's rich society, there were some of the most beautiful women, with lovely defined dark features and rich, shiny black hair. As most wore saris it was difficult to pass an opinion on their figures! Mind you blondes have always been my favourite and I've never seen a blonde Indian woman!

One thing that stands out in my memory of Bombay was in the evening when walking along the pavements you had to step over the rows of bodies lying sleeping, for the pavement was their bed for the night. Some were fortunate to have a mattress to lie on but the majority just lay on the pavement in the clothes they were wearing, using their bag of belongings as a pillow. I asked myself, is this really how the other half of the world lives?

On later trips here I did manage to visit the beautiful Phiresa Mehta Gardens which were part of the huge Kamala Nehru Park, named after ex-President Nehru's wife. Although the temperatures were always above eighty degrees, no matter when I visited these gardens, the beds of flowers and the lawns were always kept in an immaculate condition by the large number of gardeners employed to look after them. I was not a keen gardener myself then but I could appreciate the wonderful display of colour and patterned beds of flowers displayed and the beautiful green trimmed lawns. It was here in these gardens where I saw an Indian film being shot and as I understand, there were lots of films shot in these gardens, which gave an ideal background to most of their love story films. The Indian film industry is so big that it is now known as 'Bollywood'.

In one corner of the park was a stone built tower which would be about twelve feet in diameter and about thirty foot high. This tower was used by the Parsees, one of the various Indian sects, descendants of the Zoroastrians, or fire worshippers of Persia (now Iran) and who are now more numerous in India than of the old land of the Shah. They would lay the bodies of their dead inside the base of the tower and leave them there for the crows and vultures to pick and eat until only the bones remained.

My first visit to Bombay had been quite an experience but not so pleasant in the fact that there was so much poverty and sadness all around. It was not until later trips that I discovered some of the more pleasant sides to Bombay. I shall always remember Bombay, for it was there on one trip that I experienced the warmest afternoon in my life. The outside temperature was 113 degrees Fahrenheit (45 degrees Centigrade). I sat out on deck in what little shade there was unable to move, for the least bit of exertion just produced more perspiration.

Our stay in Bombay usually lasted about ten hours. We would arrive early in the morning and leave at about six in the evening, enough time for the passengers to get a taste of India and time for the ship to discharge her Royal Mail and any cargo assigned to that port. It was refreshing to be at sea once again after leaving behind the bad experiences which stick in your mind such as the poverty and sickly odours.

It was during this, my first trip, that I learned a very important lesson. Keep the galley staff happy by tending immediately to their requirements regarding maintenance and repairing their equipment on failure. Prompt attention to the galley staff requirements induces the chefs to reciprocate in offering some small mouth-watering delicacy in return, such as having a fresh bread bun plastered with butter given to you when you were working on some piece of machinery in the middle of the night on watch duty or a bowl of the chef's freshly made broth or a delicious fresh cream cake from the pastry chef, not forgetting the chef sending you a large bowl of Irish stew specially made for the crew, to your cabin. These special crew meals were always acceptable as they were tasty and wholesome - a change from the rich passenger menu food. Mind you, I'm not complaining about the passenger menus, they were excellent but it was nice to have something plain for a change.

There were times when I was about to go on leave that I could have had a joint of beef or lamb or a chicken to take home but I wouldn't take the risk of being stopped at the dock gates and my bags searched. Since that first trip, on boarding any new ship, I always quickly introduced myself to the chefs and looked after their needs, mechanically and electrically, so that my stomach would always gain. Food has always been a hobby of mine, hence my always keeping well in with the galley staff.

The weather quickly changed during the next part of our voyage to Ceylon (now Sri Lanka). Peter and I were sea-sick once more and I was now beginning to realise that sea-sickness must be the worst feeling in the world as there were times when I felt it would be better to jump overboard than suffer the constant nausea and sore stomach through continuous vomiting with nothing to bring up. This lasted for two or three days until we finally reached Colombo, the capital of Ceylon, where once again Peter and I were allowed to go ashore.

There wasn't a great lot to see in Colombo as far as I remember but it was certainly a lot cleaner than Bombay. Most buildings were painted white which gave it an air of spaciousness and brightness while most of the roads, even though they were only dirt tracks in places, were lined on either side with palm trees. The Ceylonese were very friendly and quite a few spoke good English. This was the first country where I saw and rode in a tricycle rickshaw, which was the best way of travelling and seeing the town. There was also my first encounter with a snake charmer. It fascinated me how the snake rose out of the basket at the sound of the flute type instrument being played and swayed when the charmer moved the instrument from side to side.

On a later visit to Colombo I was looking around a small gift shop when I was approached and asked to deliver some diamonds to an address in Melbourne, Australia. There was an offer of one hundred pounds if I took the parcel and another hundred pounds when I delivered it. No way was I getting involved with smuggling, particularly with diamonds even though the money was very tempting. I refused and left the shop, mystified as to why the shop proprietor should pick me out as a contraband carrier. Was it the young innocent look or did he think I needed the money? Who knows?

It wasn't until we had set sail from Colombo that I realised how he knew I was travelling to Australia: it was the all white rig-out I was wearing that gave me away and the fact that he would know that a P.& O. liner had docked that very morning.

29. Colombo to Melbourne

W̶E DEPARTED FROM COLOMBO in the evening after discharging our cargo from England and taking on a cargo of fruit and tea for Australia. The voyage down through the Indian Ocean was fairly calm and uneventful except that I got my first sighting of the Cocos or Keeling Islands which we passed fairly close to. These are a group of tropical islands owned by Australia, half way between our journey from Ceylon to Australia and how lush they looked under a clear blue sky with the sun beating down on the palm trees and the white sandy beaches. It made you feel that you wanted to get off the ship and spend some time relaxing on these paradise islands. Wishful dreaming; back to work, keeping the ship going and passengers happy.

My first thoughts on the ship's arrival at Fremantle on the western coast of Australia was; "Six weeks ago I was in London and now here I am in Australia after having sailed over ten thousand miles half way round the world" - unbelievable for a Geordie who had hardly seen much of his own country and now at last I was stepping onto Aussie soil.

Although we had docked in the port of Fremantle, most passengers and crew going ashore made their way to the capital of Western Australia, Perth, only a few miles away. Perth is situated on the estuary of the river Swan whose mouth forms the inner harbour of Fremantle. This was a well planned, beautiful garden city, well laid out to enable you to find your way around easily. There were magnificent buildings, a huge shopping area and beautiful gardens in abundance. It looked and was a very clean and well kept city, for which its inhabitants were justly proud and rightly so in my opinion.

The port of Fremantle was also the first disembarking point for some of our British emigrants. About a ten hour stay in Fremantle enabled the ship to unload passengers, Royal Mail and cargo, before we set sail for Adelaide the capital of South Australia. The journey to Adelaide was across a stretch of water known as the Great Australian Bight, famous for its rough weather. We were not disappointed for once again on my first trip we hit some of the roughest weather experienced in that part of the world for a long time. I cannot remember much about the journey but I know I was seasick all day and every day to Adelaide.

One early evening I said to Peter to try and cheer him up for he was in a worse state than me, "There's only one more thing to come up, Peter and that's the moon". Once again the indescribable feeling of nausea had me thinking "Why did I have to come to sea and oh, how I wish I were dead!"

At Adelaide we disembarked further passengers, mail and cargo. Peter and I went ashore to explore what the city had to offer. Adelaide is situated at the base of the Mount Lofty range of mountains to the east and is divided by the river Torrens. The southern side of the river is the business district while the northern side is the residential part of the city. Adelaide was very much the same as any other city but in my opinion not as nice as Perth.

On our first visit, Peter and I, would you believe it, spent most of our time in a rowing boat on the river Torrens. When I think about it now I would have thought the last place Peter and I would want to be after the rough crossing was a rowing boat. Still it was calm and we did get to see some of the more picturesque parts of the city instead of wandering around the city centre looking in shop windows.

Moving on, our next destination was the city of Melbourne, about six hundred miles from Adelaide, which thank goodness was a fairly calm journey, for by now, I wasn't feeling too good after all this sea sickness. Melbourne is the capital of the state of Victoria, which lies on the mouth of the river Yarra. It was formerly the capital of Australia.

The docks at Melbourne are a short train journey from the city, so after working on board in the morning, Peter and I, through the generosity of the chief, were allowed to take advantage of this transport and visit the city. On arrival at Flinders Street, the main city station, we were walking along the platform towards the ticket collecting barrier when I was surprised to hear the dulcet tones of a Geordie voice shouting "have ya tickets ready lads and lasses if ya please". I could not believe it, here I was over ten thousand miles from home and the first Australian I meet in Melbourne happens to be a Geordie. He got an even bigger shock when I approached him and said "Ave lost me ticket, and ave got ne money", in the best Tyneside accent I could muster. It was a few minutes before I could have a conversation with him, as he still had tickets to collect. It transpired that he had come out to Australia on the ten pounds emigration scheme three years previously, spent two years doing odd jobs all over the state and eventually finished up working for the state railways, which as he said was at least a steady job. A strange coincidence was that he had lived in the same suburb of Newcastle as I did I was at home. I knew the very street he had resided in and some of the families he knew. It's a small world.

After leaving the station Peter and I went out to explore the city. The city was very much like any other except that all Australian cities are laid out similar to the American system whereby the roads and streets run either parallel or directly at ninety degrees to one another. This makes it simple to move around and find your way easily on a street map. After visiting one or two shops we did eventually go and visit the Healesville Sanctuary which has been the traditional place to see Australian wildlife on the north eastern side of the city. It was here where we saw our first koala bear and various other Australian species of animals, birds, tropical plants and trees.

We normally spent two days in Melbourne, arriving early morning and leaving late afternoon the following day. I liked Melbourne for it was here that I used to visit relations of a lady who attended the chapel I went to back home. To visit this family I had about an hour's journey by train to the northern outskirts of the city. They were a nice family who always made me welcome and took time out to show me around the area. In return for their generous hospitality, I would arrange for them all to come to the ship and have dinner on board which always proved to be a special treat for them.

30. Melbourne to Sydney

As WE LEFT THE PORT OF MELBOURNE heading eastwards then north, the weather changed for the worst and the seven hundred mile trip to Sydney was a nightmare for me. Trying to keep food down and work at the same time must be one of the most uncomfortable experiences a person can endure, to put it mildly.

As I recall, my first sight of the bridge as we entered Sydney harbour was quite nostalgic for me, as it is a replica of the Tyne bridge, except built on a much larger scale. There the comparison ends, for Sydney harbour has to be one of the most scenic harbours in the world and this is one place I would really like to revisit.

Sydney is the capital of New South Wales lying on the shore of Port Jackson Bay with many beautiful buildings and parks stretching south to Botany Bay. A short drive from the city is the famous Bondi Beach with its white sand and enormous breakers rolling in from the Pacific Ocean, not to mention the beautiful Australian tanned 'bathing belles'!

Sydney was the city to be in for it had everything, shops, an efficient transport system, lovely parks and gardens, beautiful beaches, lots of good restaurants and pubs. Above all, the most beautiful views of the harbour, right on the city doorstep.

This was the end of the outgoing voyage for us, unless you had a round trip ticket, it was our terminus, where all passengers disembarked and we unloaded the last of our outgoing mail and most of our cargo. The ship usually stayed berthed in the dock for five days before commencing its return voyage to the UK. This gave the officers and crew ample time to explore this wonderful city and its surrounding areas.

It had been quite a unique first outward voyage for me, experiencing life as an officer on board this huge ship, making new friends, fraternising with passengers, seeing all these new countries but unfortunately worst of all, seasickness. I have to say the return voyage wasn't any easier for I was sick going across the Australian Bight again as well as the Indian Ocean, part of the Mediterranean and of course the notorious Bay of Biscay.

That first trip I lost a stone and a half in weight through seasickness. On subsequent voyages I was rarely seasick in rough weather although I could always sense when the ship was heading into rough seas for I would invariably get a headache and my stomach would feel a little queasy. This was a warning for me to keep off the rich food served in the passengers dining room and eat plenty of dry biscuits or bread to prevent me from being seasick.

I believe this was also the beginning of my experiencing migraine headaches which I suffered at least once per week for more than thirty years. I no longer get the headaches, only the warning symptoms where my vision blurs for half an hour before going back to normal. This is a nuisance at times, particularly if I'm driving, for then Joan my wife has to take over. Still its better than having the headaches.

31. Voyage Experiences

I DON'T RECALL EVERY VOYAGE I made in detail but the following are some of the more interesting events and adventures I experienced.

My third voyage out to Australia started at one o' clock in the morning. We left Tilbury Docks and I was called to my standby position which was in the main switchboard room of the machinery space. I would remain at this position until the ship was well clear of the river Thames and heading into the English Channel. Before setting off, a routine check of the machinery spaces would be made to make sure that all necessary equipment and machines were operating ready for departure. This was usually done one hour prior to departure.

Just before leaving the passenger terminal, all staff involved with the departure would be called to standby stations where they would stay until instructed to stand down by the engineer in charge at the time. My standby procedure was to view the various electrical instruments on each main switchboard and make sure that the main generators which were running in parallel were operating satisfactorily and providing enough power for the ship's requirement without getting overloaded.

One of the key features of any standby is to make sure that dual power supplies to the steering gear equipment are maintained. The ship would normally operate on one steering gear motor but under standby conditions two would be made available in case one failed.

It was about 3am before I got the signal that I could stand down and return to my bed but before doing so I went over to the starboard switchboard to isolate one of the steering gear supplies which was normal practice once standby was over. I was beginning to climb the last set of stairs leading out of the machinery space when I heard the engineers alarm sounding and suddenly I was confronted by my engineering colleagues rushing towards me. One of them shouted that the ship had lost all steering power.

I immediately went back to the main switchboard and checked the steering gear supply switches which, to my horror I found were both in the isolated position. I replaced one of the switches in the 'on' position and went down to the engine control position to report to the senior engineer on duty why the steering had failed. At the stand down signal I had gone and isolated one of the steering switches believing the other switch was closed. Unfortunately only one switch had been closed before departure.

It wasn't until I returned topside that I was informed that the ship had almost collided with a naval vessel performing exercises in the vicinity. It was only through the quick thinking of the ship's carpenter, on duty on the bow at the time, who released both anchors in order to avoid what could have resulted in a serious collision.

The following day I was escorted, in full uniform, by the chief engineer to the captain's cabin where a full enquiry was carried out as to why the ship had lost all steering power. I admitted that I had assumed that both steering gear switches were closed when I had gone on duty and that I should have checked. The captain and chief suggested that it may have been tiredness at having to go on duty at such an early hour in the morning which caused me to overlook checking that both switches were closed. I denied claiming lack of sleep had anything to do with the incident and admitted that although both of those switches should have been closed before we left port, I should have checked that was the situation. The captain was very understanding and that while he sympathised with my position on this incident he would have to send a full report to head office and with that I was excused.

The strange thing about this event was that the following trip I was promoted to assistant second electrical officer, which to me meant the company had accepted the incident as human error and above all had faith in my capabilities as an electrical officer.

At the beginning of every new voyage most of the officers looked forward to the first evening dinner for that was the opportunity to assess the form and beauty of the female talent on board, the majority of whom would be with us for the next twelve weeks. The patter between the officers on those evenings was, to say the least, most revealing and amusing, particularly when more than one officer fancied the same girl. It then became a challenge as to who could date the fancied girl first. The more bold type of officer would make his move at the first opportunity whilst the quieter and crafty ones would bide their time until the ship had rounded the Strait of Gibraltar and was heading into the warmer climate of the Mediterranean Sea.

What has climate to do with dating a girl you may ask? Well believe it or not the warmer weather used to bring all the young females out on deck in their various bathing attire with the intent of first getting a good overall tan and secondly to try and win the attention of an officer. It's amazing what a uniform can do to the female of the species, particularly when the officers are wearing their tropical white uniform and it's well known throughout the sailing fraternity that the sun nearly always arouses the ladies. The combination of both meant a very pleasant voyage for both officers and passengers!

Bearing in mind the strict company rule about not visiting a passenger's cabin unless for maintenance purposes, shipboard romances were restricted to the open decks and the dance area which was the only public area officers were allowed to use. The favourite meeting spot for couples was on the top most deck where the lighting was sparse which left plenty of dark areas for them to indulge their passion! Some of the engineering officers took a risk by inviting their chosen partner down to their cabin. This was usually done when the chief and second engineer were out of the accommodation although some were brave enough to risk it when they were there. If you were caught then it was a severe reprimand by the chief engineer and whereas some chiefs would ignore it, it certainly wasn't encouraged. Some senior officers would not object to officers entertaining ladies to a drink in their cabin before dinner, it all depended on whether the chief was a strict disciplinarian.

One voyage we were on our way across the Indian Ocean, it was the middle of the night with a choppy sea running at the time and it was very hot and humid, hence I had my porthole open with its scoop attachment to collect as much air as possible. I was sound asleep when there was an almighty thud that woke me. I got out of bed and as my feet touched the deck I realised I was standing in water. My immediate reaction was that we must be sinking, so I grabbed my life-jacket and ran into the corridor expecting to see the rest of the engineering staff but not a soul was in sight. I then noticed, to my relief, that there was no water in the corridor and crept sheepishly back to my cabin before anyone could see me. What had happened was that a freak wave had hit my side of the ship and sent water pouring through my porthole into the cabin. I smiled afterwards but at two or three o' clock in the morning, wakening out of a sound sleep and finding water in your cabin, what would you have thought?

Work on board was varied and consisted of general maintenance of all electrical machinery and equipment and the servicing and repair of passenger electric irons or telephones, etc. I was informed one day that the captain's telephone was out of order and that I had to repair the fault immediately. After knocking on the door and getting no answer I gingerly entered to find the cabin empty. The captain, being the senior in rank, had a very spacious day room, an office leading off one side and a bedroom off the other side. He had a telephone in his office and one in his bedroom. I discovered the fault was in the office telephone. After rectifying it, I started to check it by calling out "Hello" into the receiver and immediately got a reply of "Hello" but it did not seem to come from the earpiece of the phone, so I tried again and got the same response. This was getting a little baffling. This time I called out "Hello, can you hear me?" and back came the reply "Hello, can you hear me?" I was starting to get annoyed by this time, when I thought I would try the bedroom phone. Once again I went through the same procedure getting the same reply but I suddenly realised the replies were not coming from the phone but from the captain's dayroom, where on investigation, I found a large green and red feathered parrot sitting in its cage. As soon as I said "Hello" back came the reply, "Hello." I had to laugh, for I'd been taken for a ride by a bird, not for the first time I have to admit but then they were of the 'dolly bird' variety!

During one of my voyages on the "Strathmore", I made friends with an Australian engineer who everyone called Aussie Brian. He had ginger hair, was very broad shouldered and athletically built as well as being very competitive in all sporting activities. He and I got on famously for I loved any sporting activity barring cricket. It was Aussie Brian who showed me round Sydney and took me out in his car into the Blue Mountains where we visited the Jenolan Caves, a sight never to be forgotten. Then on the way back I saw my first wild wallabies and kangaroos hopping around the rugged countryside.

Aussie Brian had a girlfriend on board called Margaret Everingham who was a stenographer in the ship's bureau. Margaret was a lovely girl, she had dark hair, was medium build and always wore a lovely smile. She also had a lovely placid nature. We would all go ashore together exploring new countries and cities, each of us happy in the company of the other and in case you get the idea that three's a crowd, I was always invited to go along with them.

Margaret and I later became extremely good friends. In fact she was very much like a sister to me. We had a special relationship whereby we could talk and discuss any subject together. Some of the other officers thought there was romance between us but I can assure you it was purely a platonic friendship, for she knew that I had a girlfriend back home. If I hadn't known Joan at the time perhaps the friendship might have developed further, anyway I'm pleased it did not.

Before I first went off to sea, my relationship with Joan Lillie, my girlfriend, wasn't progressing very well. In fact we had just about finished seeing each other which in one respect was probably a good thing for it gave us both space and time to think if there was any future in it. It wasn't until a few voyages later that we got back together and started to enjoy each other's company. What is that old saying? Oh yes, 'absence makes the heart grow fonder', well it worked for us, for we decided to get engaged.

We had looked at a selection of engagement rings, when I was home on leave, so I knew the type of ring Joan wanted. I had also made note of the size of ring required. The reason for wanting to know the size of ring was because I would be able to get much better value abroad for the money I could afford to spend than I would in England.

During our stay in Sydney, the captain would hold an evening buffet supper and dance on board ship when special guests would be invited. All officers were invited to attend these occasions and were expected to accompany a partner. I thought I was going to have to decline my first invitation to the dance as I had no partner, but the more experienced officers wouldn't hear of this. They informed me that on the evening of the dance there would be a partner for me and for those others who had no one to escort.

Apparently if there were partners required, one of the officers would ring up the local hospital and arrange for the required number of nurses to attend. I understand there were always plenty of volunteers.

The dance commenced without my intended partner having turned up but I was assured by one of the other nurses that she would eventually attend after finishing her duty shift. The announcement that the buffet was now being served broke the spell of my boredom at not being able to dance. I was about to leave for the buffet when a voice behind me said in a strong Australian accent "Hello Ken, I'm Pat, I'm your partner for this evening". I turned to find this chubby young nurse with dark curly hair and a very tanned, smiling face.

My immediate thought was that I'd drawn the short straw, however her redeeming feature was that she was in Aussie terms 'a hell of a good dancer'! The evening went well after the introductions even though it was sometimes a battle to get my arm round her when dancing. With a crowd of about ten of us at one table it turned out a better evening than I had imagined. When the nurses left, we officers continued with the party in one of the purser's cabins, where all kinds of sea shanties were rendered and party tricks displayed, the likes of which I could not reveal here.

The following trip into Sydney I received a phone call from Pat asking me to see her but I declined. I didn't want to get involved and anyway I had Margaret my stenographer friend lined up for the captain's buffet dance. While on the subject of dancing, one evening at sea, all available officers were summoned to attend the ship's dance floor as there was a shortage of gentlemen on board. Can you believe it, being ordered to dance with the ladies? We thought it some prank being played by the deck officers but no, it was true. The dance was in full swing by the time a few of my fellow officers and I arrived. That particular night there was a gentle swell on the sea which made the ship roll very slightly but did not stop the dancing.

After standing eyeing up the talent, I decided to ask one lady for a dance. She was nothing special to look at but I knew she was a good dancer having watched her on previous evenings. She was built like my boyhood favourite film star Jane Russell (for the uninitiated that means she was a 38 inch cup). We started to dance and had circled the floor quite a few times when all of a sudden a freak wave hit the ship broadside on and she heeled over about twenty five degrees. All the dancers finished up on one side of the dance floor in what can only be described as a pile of bodies. I was fortunate for I landed on top of my partner, who as I said, was well cushioned with my head cradled nicely somewhere soft! We all lay there for a while recovering from the shock, before attempting to move and discover if any one had suffered injury. I could have stayed there longer, for I was listening to see if I could hear my partner's heartbeat, for she had fallen heavily. As an officer and a gentleman I jumped up and assisted the ladies to their feet and fortunately there were no casualties. After that experience, there was a big demand to dance with Jane Russell, particularly if the ship was rolling!

One voyage we had a group of about six Australian girls travelling out to Australia with us who became friendly with some of the engineering staff. We used to entertain them most nights with drinks before dinner, then afterwards dancing or whatever entertainment was going on in the dance area or just sit and chat together. On arrival in Sydney, the girls all left the ship having said their goodbyes the previous evening. The next day we all received an invitation from the mother of one of the girls to attend an evening at the cinema, followed by supper at the mother's home. Those of us who could, for two of the engineers were on duty watch that night, went along and had a great evening's entertainment and supper followed by dancing in what must have been the largest house in Sydney. Just before we left, the mother made a little speech, thanking us for entertaining the girls on voyage and said that she had wanted to show her gratitude by arranging the evening's entertainment for us. That wasn't the end of her gratitude though for we were all invited to her beach house for lunch the following day which was fortunately a Sunday, my day off duty.

The beach house was a huge bungalow positioned alongside the sea front where we all enjoyed the company of our host and the girls before the morning culminated with a delicious picnic lunch on the beach. It wasn't until we were about to leave that I discovered from one of the other girls that the mother, who had lavishly entertained us, was the wife of the managing director of the Kiwi Boot Polish Company. Despite her social status and busy lifestyle, she had still found time to show us her gratitude for entertaining her daughter and friends on board the ship. She was just one of a number of very kind Australian people I met.

While the ship was docked in Sydney, the second engineer and one of the deck officers would arrange for those off duty to have a trip in one of the ships lifeboats to one of the many picturesque spots in and around Sydney Harbour. I went on a few of these trips and thoroughly enjoyed them for it gave you the opportunity to see the surrounding area of the harbour.

One trip we went up one of the small tributaries flowing into the harbour and found a nice spot to tie up and have our picnic. We had to tie up at this point as the water was getting quite shallow down to a couple of feet or more. After satisfying our hunger the men decided to play football. Just across from where we had parked the boat was a small island and one of our enthusiastic colleagues hit the ball onto this island. One of our group was about to cross the shallow water to retrieve the ball when a strong Aussie voice shouted out "Don't go in the water Cobber, it's crawling with crocodiles!". On closer examination of the island's water edge we could see some of them lying there, looking like floating logs. The Aussie passer-by assured us that if our friend had ventured in he would have been a 'gonner' for sure. Our volunteer was grateful to say the least and pretty shaken, as we all were, at the thought of what could have happened.

Another occasion, we set off in the lifeboat for a trip and headed towards the mouth of the harbour with the intention of visiting the famous Bondi Beach. As we neared the mouth of the harbour the water started to get a little rough and I and a few others were starting to feel a little queasy. The second engineer who was in charge obviously realised that some of us were under the weather and diplomatically suggested that it was too rough to go out of the harbour and that he was turning the boat around. It was at this point that I became aware of some very large objects swimming alongside and around the boat. When I pointed this out to the others an immediate cry bellowed out from one of the mates, "Sharks!". Without any hesitation I moved into the centre of the boat, trembling with fear at the thought of them overturning the boat and the realisation that I couldn't swim very well, not that it would have made any difference! By this time two of the stenographer ladies in the party were also beginning to panic and it was only the smooth assurance of the senior mate that all was well as long as we stayed calm. The girls and I found this very hard to do and didn't relax until we were well clear of the harbour and heading up one of the small estuaries where the waters were much calmer and well away from the sharks. That trip taught me a lesson for from that day on, I vowed I would never swim in Australian waters even though at times when I was on the beach the sea would be very inviting. I never succumbed to the temptation even though there were nets placed fifty or more yards out to sea to prevent the sharks entering the swimming area. The constant reminder of seeing those sharks in the harbour made sure of that!

I found the Australian people generally friendly although one or two disliked the Pommies (their name for all the English) and at every opportunity would verbally run them down. I don't think they could accept that their ancestors were British convicts! I liked them for the ones I met were friendly, honest in their opinions and always ready to find an excuse to have fun and party. Their language at times contained swear words in almost every other sentence but was accepted by them as part of their common dialogue which you became used to, for there was no malice behind it. The only thing I could not get used to was the way a lot of the Aussie women used to swear. I have never been impressed by any woman who swears, it sounds so common and rough and not a bit ladylike. Nevertheless, it was part of their vocabulary and you became used to it and not all Aussie women swore - they were in the minority.

At the end of each voyage when the ship returned to Tilbury Docks, she would stay there for about fourteen days. This was the opportunity to get major repairs attended to and to reload the vessel with supplies. Half the crew would go on leave for the first week and the rest the second week which meant there was always someone on board as standby for general duties and maintenance work. I could never decide whether it was best to take the first or second leave, for it was nice to leave the ship immediately she had docked but I was never keen to spend another week working in dock when returning from first leave. After a while it made no difference as long as I got leave.

32. A New Route

I T WAS ON MY THIRD TRIP returning from Australia when I was carrying out my usual early morning duties that I noticed that the sun was rising on the port side of the ship when it should have been rising on the starboard side. I went up to the bridge and enquired why we were heading south instead of north. They informed me that they had received a message from head office telling them to change course and head home round the Cape of South Africa because the Suez Canal had been closed. I was delighted with this news, not because they had closed the canal, but this opened up another opportunity for me to visit a country which I had only previously read about. It also changed my plan with respect to purchasing the engagement ring.

The closing of the canal became known as the Suez Crisis. It was a crucial juncture in the history of the Middle East, precipitated on 26 July 1956, when Gamen Abdel Nasser, the Egyptian leader, nationalised the Suez Canal. The crisis was provoked by the American and British decision not to finance the construction of the Aswan dam as they had promised and against the response to the growth of Egypt's affinity with Czechoslovakia and the Soviet Union. Nasser reacted by declaring martial law in the Canal Zone and seized control of the Canal Company.

Our ship was one of the last vessels to pass south through the canal. A change of course meant that we now sailed south through the Indian Ocean hugging the African coast. We passed the Seychelle Islands, Mozambique and the island of Madagascar, eventually arriving at the port of Durban situated on the south western coast of South Africa. I do not recall a great deal about Durban as a city but I do remember being aware that I was in a country that was steeped in racism. On the seafront were seats reserved only for white people and separate public toilets for both white and black people. There were also segregated compartments on the public transport and it was obvious that only the black people were employed to do the menial tasks. Up to that time I had not thought a great deal about apartheid. But when you witness it happening in everyday life then your conscience is pricked and you get a nauseating feeling in the pit of your stomach and start to realise the deprivation and humiliation suffered by these people.

While we were berthed in Durban the passengers were entertained by a dozen or more Zulu warriors dancing various ritual dances in their native dress. This was a sight to behold for each man was over seven feet tall and all wearing the most colourful head-dress and loin cloth you could ever wish to see, a really spectacular display that I and the passengers were pleased to have witnessed.

The morning of departure from Durban was quite dramatic for there was a gale blowing out at sea. Whether it was because we had a time schedule to keep I'm not sure but our captain gave the order to sail. We got out of Durban harbour safely and into some very rough sea. On our normal journeys between ports we would cruise at a speed of around eighteen knots (approximately 21mph) but today that wasn't going to be possible. For one thing, the waves were quite large and threatening, so much so, that we dared not go broadside on to them without the fear of the vessel rolling to one side and never recovering her state of equilibrium. Hence we headed into the waves which unfortunately made the ship pitch and roll unceasingly. The more we neared the notorious Cape Horn the worse the weather got and our speed was reduced to a mere six knots and even with our stabilisers operating they made little difference to the movement of the vessel. It was when we were at the tip of the Cape where the South Atlantic Ocean converges with the Indian Ocean that the weather worsened and waves the height of two story buildings were raining down on the bow and forward hatches even up to the wheelhouse windows. I have never seen the sea so rough but strange as it may seem, I was not seasick. At last I could claim to be a hardened sailor!

Most of the passengers had retired to their cabins whilst the hardy few sat in the lounges nervously hanging on to their seats as the ship pitched and rolled. It got so bad that the captain came off the bridge to reassure the passengers that everything was under control and that we'd soon be in Cape Town. We arrived in Cape Town at seven in the morning, about eighteen hours late, where we tied up in the harbour beneath the famous Table Mountain which made a very impressive back drop in the early morning sun.

Most of the passengers went ashore, mainly to find their 'land legs' after a most uncomfortable journey round the Cape. Margaret, Aussie Brian and I went ashore and after exploring the city for a while went and got the cable car to the top of Table Mountain where we experienced the most magnificent views. The view was something to behold and I never forgot that experience. In the afternoon I left Margaret and Brian to do their own thing and went off looking for a good jeweller's shop. It didn't take long for once in the middle of the city there were plenty to choose from. After a couple of hours viewing various engagement rings I eventually settled on one which fitted the description Joan and I had agreed on. The solitaire diamond, I was told, had been mined from a South African diamond mine near Johannesburg. That was good enough for me, for with its English value double the amount I paid in Cape Town, I reckoned I had chosen wisely and felt sure Joan would like it. Mind you it would have been hard lines if she hadn't!

From Cape Town we headed north up the West African coast to the port of Dakar in the province of Senegal. All I remember about Dakar was that it appeared dirty and dusty with an abundance of flies everywhere. The people were all very tall, even the women were well over six feet and most of the men seven foot tall, my six foot four inches seemed small amongst them!

Our final destination was the port of Las Palmas on the island of Gran Canaria, in the Canary Isles. The island had some beautiful beaches and plenty of souvenir shops but as we were only there for half a day I didn't see much else.

A few days later we entered the English Channel and thick fog. Even with all the modern radar aids, it's a most uncomfortable feeling moving through dense fog with the booming sound of the ship's siren every two minutes. I was never happy in this situation for I always feared the possibility of a collision with another vessel. Our ship had left the English Channel and was just entering the Thames estuary when my worst fears came true. I happened to be out on deck leaning over the aft starboard rail looking to see if the fog was lifting when all of a sudden out of the mist I could see the bow of another ship heading towards our bow which meant a certain collision.

Our ship immediately steered to port which prevented a head on collision but did not prevent the other vessel scraping along our starboard side and tearing away the passenger gangway stowed on the side of our vessel. The collision had been with a Norwegian cargo vessel named 'Baalbek' just off Gravesend at the mouth of the river. A fitting name to a spot that could have witnessed a fatal disaster had both vessels not been travelling at a reduced speed in the fog.

This particular trip from Australia to England was unusual in that we crossed the equator three times and steamed a total of 17,410 miles which took fifty one days to complete. A souvenir card was printed on board commemorating the voyage and was issued to all the passengers. The round trip from London for the officers and crew covered about 30,000 miles and we crossed the equator four times, a record for a single voyage.

Having arrived back in Tilbury Docks I was on first leave so I was off the ship by mid morning and on my way home after safely getting through customs without having a body search, for I was carrying the engagement ring wrapped in a handkerchief tucked into my underpants. It was with a sigh of relief that I also passed through the dock entrance gates without being body searched, although they did search my travel bag. It was the one and only time that I had not declared an item I had bought abroad and I vowed there and then never to go through the customs inspection trauma again trying to hide something on my person. The customs inspectors were pretty thorough in searching crew cabins at that time and would think nothing of removing panels and cupboards in the hope of finding illegal contraband. Each member of the crew was allowed to bring ashore a bottle of spirits and two hundred cigarettes. The cigarettes were two old shillings and sixpence per tin of fifty and a bottle of whisky cost about two pounds, old money. I used to take my allocation of cigarettes and spirit home for my sister and brother in law who both indulged; sometimes I'd leave a bottle at home for use at Christmas when we had visitors.

If the customs decided to pay a visit to your cabin you had to declare the goods you were taking home and if it was a bottle of spirit then it had to be opened and the neck portion drunk or removed from it. In my case the bottle was never opened for I disliked the stuff, so the customs official would open the bottle and pour the equivalent of a double whisky down the sink then replace the cork which now meant the bottle could be taken ashore. Why that amount of spirit was removed from the bottle I can only assume was to comply with some government regulation at the time. It did not matter to me but the hardened drinkers just about cried to see it being poured down the drain, when they had forgotten to drink it before the customs arrived.

I had a further voyage round the Cape to Australia both outward and homeward before the Suez Canal was reopened and we were the first vessel allowed to pass through it again. The Egyptians had cleared those parts of the canal where passage had to be made but there were signs of sunken vessels protruding out of the water at the Port Said entry and the Bitter Lakes, a sad reminder of a conflict which went badly wrong for Britain.

After five voyages to Australia and back I left the 'Strathmore' to take a few months leave which I had accrued since joining the company. While sea life was good, I always enjoyed going home to see my mother, sisters and my girlfriend Joan, who by this time, had now become my fiancée. When mother knew I was coming home, she always prepared a tea of corned beef, newly baked bread buns and pickled onions, for this was my favourite tea. It was also a delight to be eating stew and dumplings for dinner once more; good plain wholesome food, you can't beat it. A delicious change from the very rich food I had been eating on board.

It was at sea that I taught myself letter writing for I sent Joan a letter and my mother an air-mail letter from every port. Hence I received two letters per port which were greatly appreciated. Letter writing reminds me of the Tyneside mother's letter to her son at sea.

Dear Son,

Just a few lines to let you know I am still alive. I am writing this letter slowly cos I know you can't read very fast. You won't know the house when you come home – we've moved. About your father, he's got a lovely new job. He has about five hundred men under him – he's cutting the grass in the cemetery.

There was a washing machine in the new house when we moved in, but it's not working too good. Last week I put fourteen shirts into it, pulled the chain and haven't seen them since. Your sister Mary had a baby this morning but I haven't found out whether it's a boy or girl yet so I don't know if you're an uncle or an aunt.

Your Uncle Mick drowned last week in a vat of whisky at Newcastle Breweries. Some of his work mates dived in to save him but he fought them off bravely. We cremated his body and it took three days for the fire to go out. Your father didn't have much to drink at Christmas. I put a bottle of castor oil in his brown ale. It kept him going till New Year's Day.

I went to see the doctor on Thursday, your father came with me. The doctor put a small glass tube in my mouth and told me not to open it for ten minutes. Your father offered to buy it off him.

It rained twice last week; first for three days, then for four days. Monday was so windy that one of the chickens laid the same egg four times. We had a letter from the undertaker, he says if we don't pay the last instalment on your granny – up she comes.

That's all for now.

P.S. I was going to send you £10 but I'd already sealed the letter.

Love, Mother.

Thankfully not all Tyneside mothers send their sons such interesting letters.

33. Route to the Orient

ON RETURN FROM LEAVE, I worked at the docks for a few weeks on various
P. & O liners doing maintenance work. Eventually I was appointed as second
electrical officer on the S. S. Carthage voyaging to Hong Kong and back; a
round trip of about ten weeks. The ship derived its name from the ancient
Tunisian city of Carthage which was a rival to the Republic of Rome in earlier
times. She was a 14,304 gross tons passenger liner built at Alexander Stephen &
Sons shipyard Glasgow in 1931. Her propulsion was by twin screws, powered
from engines which comprised of six single reduction geared steam turbines
that gave her a cruising speed of 18 knots. There were 279 in her crew and she
could accommodate 177 first class and 214 second class passengers.

It was P. & O. custom that no electrical officer could be promoted to chief
without first spending a number of voyages on one or more of the P. & O.
cargo ships. Having done his service on cargo vessels this entitled him to be
promoted to chief. He could then continue to serve on cargo vessels and wait
until a vacancy occurred on one of the passenger liners.

Promotion to chief electrical engineering officer on any P. & O. liner was
achieved by your length of service within the company. I did not want to leave
the liners, life was good so I never reached the dizzy heights of 'chief'.

The voyage out to Hong Kong covered the same route as the Australian
voyage except from Colombo we headed east to Penang then south to
Singapore before heading north east to Hong Kong.

There were only three electrical officers on the 'Carthage', a chief named

Ron Ellis who was an Irishman, a second, yours truly, and a third called Harry Shimmen from Essex. Ron was a character, typical Irish with his outlandish statements, weird jokes and his ability to make you think he was working hard when in fact he did very little. For all that you couldn't help liking him for he was so cheerful and the life and soul of any party. Harry was totally different to Ron, he was much younger and had a happy-go-lucky attitude to life which made him popular with the rest of the officers. He was a competent electrical officer who could be relied on at all times and during our voyages to the Far East together we became very good friends. There was also an assistant engineer on board called Mike Bowker, a Lancashire lad from Blackburn who became good friends with Harry and me. Mike was a determined character who knew what he wanted and where he was going and nothing was going to prevent him achieving that. He was also full of fun, a prankster and enjoyed his drink.

With Harry's happy outlook and Mike's fun loving attitude and my combination of the two blended with a little more sobriety, we made a perfect trio. This relationship found no barriers in the close friendship we shared. I can honestly say that the voyages spent with Harry and Mike were some of the most enjoyable times I experienced at sea.

My first trip to the far east after visiting Colombo became more exciting for me as we were now visiting new ports of call, namely, Penang, Singapore and finally Hong Kong. On leaving Colombo in Ceylon we sailed east across the Indian Ocean rounding the northern point of Sumatra into the Straight of Malacca arriving at Penang. Penang is a small island off the mainland of Malaya and was formerly known as Prince of Wales Island, a British settlement up to 1946 when it was declared a free port. Its capital is Georgetown and that was the place to visit during our short stay there.

I don't recall anything of specific interest happening here, all I remember is that it was always hot and like most eastern towns the buildings were all painted white which reflected the sun strongly and forced most of the public to wear sunglasses. Its one redeeming feature was that it had beautiful beaches and a very warm sea to swim in, a nice place for a relaxing holiday.

Leaving Penang, we headed south to Singapore, an island at the southern extremity of the Malaya Peninsular. Singapore was separated from the Malaysian mainland by the Jahore Strait and at that time the only means of communication with the mainland was by ferry. Nowadays it is linked to the mainland by a causeway. The population in those days was about two million and it has almost doubled in the last fifty years. On the south coast of Singapore was a natural harbour where the docks and the main passenger terminal were situated. Close by was the British naval base where many naval ships were berthed, some undergoing repairs and the rest ready to sail on manoeuvres or into action. Looking south from the port the whole area was dotted with beautiful tropical islands some of which could be visited by boat.

The city of Singapore was split into three areas, the business section, the shopping section and the markets, but with all three partly merging into each other. The famous street for all to visit in Singapore was known as Buggy Street where you could purchase anything and I mean anything. Mind, you had to barter for every purchase. Even for the women if you were so inclined but that was part of the fun, purchasing at a price you were happy with. At night the market stalls were all lit up with brightly coloured lights and stayed open until midnight. Among the many stalls were eating places where you could feast on the local dishes for under a pound old money. You had to be careful with hygiene although thankfully my colleagues and I never suffered any discomfort from such meals.

On my first visit to Singapore, the officers were invited to play one of the local schools at football. The game was to be played in the afternoon as that was the only time we could manage to raise a full team. Buckets of iced orange juice were placed along each side of the pitch for anyone who needed it during the game. It was certainly needed for we played in a temperature of 92 degrees and very high humidity. I survived the first twenty minutes before having to leave the field to regurgitate the lunch I had consumed earlier. I did return to play and was thankful, as all our team were, that the referee decided to cut the second half of the match by half. This was because of the excessive heat and to save our team from further embarrassment for the young thirteen year old schoolboys were winning twelve goals to two. Not a particularly enjoyable afternoon!

I had dinner that evening for I was starving after having lost my lunch at the football field. Dinner, like the lunch, was a chinese meal. Two hours after the meal I was bringing it all up again. It was not until the following day after diagnosing what I had eaten the previous day that I realised I was allergic to shellfish. There had been prawns in the lunch soup and crab in the dinner main course, both of which I had never eaten in the past. I have tried a few times over the years to see if I have overcome the allergy but to no avail.

It was in Singapore that on one trip we had our boiler maker engineer put ashore. Terry was a very heavy drinker and most evenings he would be well-oiled if not drunk. This drinking episode went on for a few trips before the alcohol began to affect his health. He began to experience hallucinations where he would see dogs following him wherever he went. One afternoon he had gone ashore into Singapore on his own. Later that afternoon a few of the duty engineering staff and I were leaning on the ship's rail watching all that was taking place on the jetty when we spotted Terry running towards the ship. He ran up the gangway which was just alongside where we were standing and on seeing us began to shout something about being chased. We realised something was wrong, grabbed hold of him and tried to calm him down, without success for he was continuously shouting "Get the dogs off me!" and kicking his feet out at imaginary barking dogs. We found out later from the doctor on board that he had gone into the city and had a heavy drinking session. After being removed from one of the bars he had set off running back to the ship which must have been all of two miles or more, thinking that he was being chased by dogs. After consultation with the chief engineer, the doctor declared him unfit for work and he was put ashore until the next P. & O. ship called to take him back to the UK where I believe he was dismissed from the company. A sad ending to Terry's career, for he was a friendly and likeable guy when sober.

On one occasion we departed Singapore with a high ranking, government official on board. He was so important that we were escorted out of the harbour by six British Royal Naval destroyers all in a line, equal distance apart, ahead of us. Then after about a mile from the harbour they stopped in one straight line while our ship sailed passed each of them saluting us with sharp blasts on their sirens. What a spectacle that was, we were proud to be British.

Singapore was always hot and sticky, you could shower four or five times during the day and still not feel cool. The problem was that it had such a high humidity factor. Although I liked Singapore very much, I was always glad to leave the sticky heat behind.

Sailing north through the South China Sea, we finally reached our Far Eastern destination namely, Hong Kong, an island situated off the mainland of China. Hong Kong, whose name means 'fragrant harbour' is one of the most exciting places in the far east. As well as being the most densely populated and one of the most cosmopolitan cities in the world, it boasts a spectacular setting. Although our itinerary stated that our terminal port was Hong Kong, the ship actually tied up at a terminal situated on the mainland of China known as Kowloon. Hong Kong was just a short ferry crossing from the mainland and is one of the most fascinating cities in the world. In the 1950's when I visited the city, there was only one sky-scraper on the island. Since then of course, having built on every piece of available land across the island the only way to expand was up-over and that's the way it is today. Hong Kong has one of the most fascinating and beautiful views from its highest mountain, known as the Peak. Its full name is Victoria Peak and it rises to 1,880ft (554m) above sea level and offers a 360 degree view of virtually the whole territory. It overlooks the harbour and mainland and on a clear day you could see the border of mainland China. So much has changed since the fifties.

The ship stayed in Hong Kong for four or five days during which we would catch up with maintenance work. Parts of the ship were repainted here for materials and labour were so cheap. The Chinese painters never used brushes to paint the vessel, they would get a piece of absorbent rag in one hand and dip it into the paint pot right up to their wrist and proceed to paint. It was an unusual method of painting but it was fast and cheap. All the teak outside decks were scrubbed down by Chinese women who would squat down all in a straight line and rub the deck with an abrasive stone back and forward slowly moving forward together occasionally splashing water over the deck where they were scrubbing. Each woman would be dressed in a black cotton type outfit or I should say uniform, comprising a pair of flared trousers and a loose fitting jacket buttoned all the way up to the neck. The women, aged anywhere between fifteen and sixty years for they all looked the same, would squat for hours on end slowly moving forward like black caterpillars with their arched backs and arms pushing and pulling the stone they held in both hands. Only they would know the pain they must have suffered by the end of the day and all for just a pittance. Their labours were not in vain for the end result was gleaming, almost white teak decks which were always admired by the passengers.

Hong Kong was a shopper's paradise for everything cost so little. Trades men and woman would come on board and attempt to sell their wares to the ship's crew. One day I decided to have a new pair of shoes, hand made. The shoemaker asked me to stand in my stocking feet on a piece of brown paper and proceeded to draw round the perimeter of my feet with a crayon, this completed he then left. Twenty four hours later he returned with my shoes made and I have to admit they were one of the most comfortable pair of shoes I have worn and they only cost me about two pounds in old money. He must have worked all night to get the shoes finished in such a short a time.

Even the tailor would make a suit for you within three days. The first day he would measure you and commence the cutting out and sewing, on the second day you would try on the suit and any adjustments were made. The third day the tailor would return with a perfectly fitting suit. Amazingly clever with their hands, these Chinese.

I have always enjoyed bartering over the price you are prepared to pay for goods and still do today in certain countries. On board the ship we would swap goods with the Chinese. There used to be an old Chinese lady come on board every trip and she would want to swap a thin cotton hand towel for a bar of soap or any fruit or sweets we had in the cabin. I always felt sorry for her and gave her as much as I could spare but she would insist I take a hand towel; I had quite a collection by the time I left sea.

Shopping ashore was an experience for the place was crammed with small shops selling everything you can think of. Bargains at that time were cameras, watches, china and beautiful silk and cotton material, apart from canaries and parrots which could be purchased 'cheeply'! Had I known at the time, I would have purchased more chinaware and household goods for Joan and me for our future house.

One day I was walking along a street in Hong Kong, when I saw a parrot in a cage. The parrot looked at me and much to my surprise, said "wot cheor Geordie, a knaa ye". "By gosh", I thought to myself. A parrot that talks Geordie, I'll buy it for my mother. She'll be over the moon with that. I went inside the shop and said to the old Chinaman behind the counter, "how much do you want for that parrot, it talks my language?" "Velly solly", says the old Chinaman "pallot not for sale, but I have egg from pallot". "Okay, I'll take the egg" I replied. The next trip, I was walking down the same street in Hong Kong, same shop, same parrot. The parrot looks at me and says, "wot cheor kiddar, I knaa ye". "Aye," I said, "A knaa ye an all, yer father was a duck!"

Harry, Mike and I never tired of wandering round Hong Kong, particularly off the main streets, exploring the dark alleyways seeing how the other half lived, it was fascinating. During the afternoon usually the hottest part of the day, we would require refreshment to cool off, so we would venture into one of the many small bars, scattered all over the city. These bars consisted of a long rectangular room with the entrance at one end and the drinks bar at the other and on either side cubicle type seats for about eight people, leaving a wide alleyway in the centre. You weren't allowed to go to the bar to get a drink, you had to sit in one of the cubicles and wait until a young Chinese girl would come and take your order. Once your order had been taken then a number of other girls dressed in 'chongsons', (tight fitting dresses with a split up each side to the waist) would, uninvited, come and sit alongside each person and in their best broken English attempt to get into conversation, get a drink bought and eventually a dance in the wide alleyway. If you weren't interested then you tried to ignore them or tell them to leave. It was difficult to find a bar where you could go in and have a quiet drink without being pestered by these girls most of whom you wouldn't look at once never mind twice, at least that's my story! The only solution was to drink in a hotel where they were not allowed to join your company unless invited. Mind, if you liked dancing then it was a cheap afternoon's outing for the drinks cost little.

In Kowloon, Mike and I went out one evening for a meal and entertainment. We arrived at one of the more select night-clubs in the city to find entry being refused by the doorman because we were not wearing a tie. It did not cross our minds to wear a tie as it was such a warm evening. This was our first experience of being refused entry anywhere on our travels. We should have known better being officers and gentlemen!

A taxi was hailed to take us back to the ship where bow ties were procured then back to the night-club for an elegant entry past a most startled doorman. We must have looked smart or wealthy for we were ushered to a front of stage table where for the rest of the evening we enjoyed a delicious meal, good wine and fine entertainment and we were not even accosted by young females; we must have been drunk!

I recall at that period of time Mike telling me that he had led a very sheltered life at home living alone with his mother. Girls had not been of interest to him. All that was to change one evening on a later trip which although very amusing, I cannot record here.

Local transport was either by taxi or by rickshaw. The rickshaws could convey one or two passengers and were always pulled by the skinniest of Chinamen. One evening Harry, Mike and I had been out for a meal at a restaurant and were about to hail a taxi when daredevil Mike, a little the worse for drink, suggested we all go back to the ship in our own individual rickshaw and see who arrives back first. Harry, always game for a laugh, thought it a good idea but then suggested we pull our own rickshaw with the Chinaman seated inside and race each other back to the ship. I wasn't too sure about this idea and I don't think the Chinamen liked it either but with the promise of extra Hong Kong dollars at the end, they quickly relented.

All three of us lined up, each with our driver apprehensively sitting in the rickshaw. We set off at a fairly quick pace. Fortunately there was not a great deal of traffic so late at night so we had a fairly clear run along a slightly inclined road. The incline proved to be steeper than we thought for the pace suddenly slowed down from trotting to walking, with Harry leading, then Mike followed by yours truly. There were some funny looks and expressions of surprise from the few pedestrians we passed on our way. Pulling a rickshaw is a work of art. For if you are clever, once you are in motion then with a little skilful balancing you can lift your feet off the ground holding the pulling shafts in each hand with your elbows lying vertical along them and let the rickshaw carry you along on its momentum. By the time we reached the top of the gradient we were all puffing and panting much to the amusement of our passengers. The real fun started when we got over the crest of the gradient for on the other side was a slight hill leading down to the waterfront where the road turned right back to the ship which was about fifty yards further on.

By now we were all very confident at pulling a rickshaw or so we thought. Mike set off at a terrific pace down the hill closely followed by Harry and me. With my long strides, I went into the lead and a quarter of the way down the hill thought I would show the other two how skilful I was at handling a rickshaw. I proceeded to balance my body weight through my arms which were now extended along each shaft and lifting my feet off the ground. You had to keep lowering the feet to the ground and run for a while otherwise the rickshaw would become uncontrollable the faster it went when free-wheeling. Not to be outdone by me the other two quickened their pace caught up and passed me; now it was their turn to show their prowess in the art and control of rickshaw driving.

Harry was the first to raise his feet off the ground and attempt to balance his weight on the shafts. He went smoothly at first but unfortunately went too close to the kerb, hit it with one wheel and overturned the rickshaw throwing the poor driver out onto the road. Mike in the meantime not to be outdone lifted his feet off the ground and instead of balancing his weight on the shafts, he somehow sent the rickshaw up in the air and back-over. The body of the rickshaw was now scraping along the ground with the Chinaman lying on his back clinging on for his life and Mike stuck up in the air with his feet dangling between the shafts frantically trying to right it.

Following close behind, I had to do an emergency stop which then propelled my passenger straight out of the rickshaw on top of me. If this had been on film we would have got an Oscar for our performances. Fortunately no one was hurt and we headed back to the ship with the correct drivers. We paid the drivers well for their nightmarish experience but they vowed that they would never let us ride in their rickshaws again. Still it was good fun and a thrilling experience.

On the other side of Hong Kong Island was a fishing village called Aberdeen. Here you could purchase all types of fish, most of which I had never heard of. This was a favourite haunt of the trio not only for tasting the different types of fish but also looking for bargains in the huge open-air market opposite the waterfront. Permanently anchored in the bay at Aberdeen was a large floating up-market restaurant boat named 'Jumbo' which served the most exotic and delicious fish dishes one could wish for. The whole of the ship, which consisted of three or four decks, was all lavishly decorated in Chinese style and fully illuminated all over with Chinese lanterns - a sight not to be missed at night.

Eating out was always a good laugh with Harry and Mike for apart from the jokes and wise cracks, there was the very unprofessional way we used chopsticks. Knives and forks were never provided in some of the top restaurants so we could spend anywhere up to four hours eating a Chinese meal and that was only the main course! Throughout my travels some of the best meals I have eaten were in Hong Kong and Kowloon.

One of the fascinating things about the harbour in Hong Kong is the constant movement of the junk boats and sanpans going about their business.

The junks were large flat-bottomed Chinese sea-going boats which carried numerous types of cargo around the coasts and seas of China and Japan. They carried large masts to accommodate the sails they used to propel the vessel; they also had a small diesel engine for manoeuvring and used this when there was little or no wind blowing. The aft end of the vessel was the living quarters where up to three or more families lived. The men would handle the cargo and operate the ship while the women would do the cleaning, washing and looking after the children. Apart from collecting food and essentials, some of the families would never be off the vessel from one year to another.

The sanpan was a much smaller vessel not much bigger than a rowing boat. It would be open except for the bow end which would be covered and this would be the family sleeping area. These little vessels would frequently come alongside the passenger ships attempting to sell the various fruit and souvenirs they carried on board. They were also travelling shops for the junk boats. Families lived on board these tiny vessels all the year round, sometimes even years without coming ashore. It was a fascinating sight to see them all scurrying about the harbour during the day, then all tie up along side each other in the evening at their reserved section of harbour jetty at Kowloon.

I must emphasise that Hong Kong is a must on anyone's list of places to visit. It was at that time a thriving, bustling city and a shopper's paradise. I never got tired of visiting this part of the world as it was so exciting and the Chinese people so friendly and welcoming.

34. Insects and Gala Evenings

ONE OF THE MOST unpleasant things about the 'Carthage' was that she was infested with cockroaches. For most of the trip the Goanese cabin boys spent a considerable amount of their time trying to get rid of these horrible little creatures with insect killer spray but to no avail. They were brown in colour and anywhere up to an inch or more in length. They could survive extreme temperatures both hot and cold. I once found some crawling all over a block of ice in the Mess-room cold box.

On one occasion I was informed that the dining room revolving doors leading from the galley into the dining room were inoperative. On checking the controller I found, on taking the cover off, hundreds of cockroaches breeding in the bottom of the cable entry box. The next five minutes was spent trampling these termites to death as quickly as possible before they got into the galley area and into the food. Fortunately I never heard of any passenger complaining about them but I'm sure they must have been aware of them.

Each time we arrived back at London Docks the ship was fumigated throughout but a few managed to survive and start off the breeding cycle once more. It could have been worse, they could have been rats! Talking about insects, there was one trip we were carrying bananas in the hold immediately outside the engineers' accommodation and two colleagues and I were standing chatting alongside the hold when out from underneath the hatch cover crawled a huge spider, at least four inches long. As we were all only wearing flip-flops no one would stand on it so I raced into my cabin got hold of one of my engine room shoes and returned to face the foe. By this time it had moved quickly towards the side of the engineers' accommodation and was about to climb up the bulkhead just beneath the porthole of my cabin. This was too much for me, down came the heavy shoe and that was the end of our giant hairy spider. One of the passengers close by reckoned it was a tarantula which would have come aboard with the bananas. Needless to say if it had got to the UK it would not have survived the climate, so perhaps I did it a favour!

Gala evenings on board ship were special for the chefs excelled themselves with a parade and display of the most exotic culinary delights to suit all palates. Party hats were the order of the evening and woe betide any officer refusing to wear one throughout the evening. After dinner everyone would make their way to the ballroom where dancing would take place until the early hours of the morning. In the interval there would be presentations for the winners of the fancy dress competition which always followed a theme selected by the staff commander. Some of the creations were very colourful and imaginative. Champagne flowed throughout the evening making the gala a happy and memorable occasion for all even though the following morning had to be faced!

35. Alarm

I HAVE ALWAYS STATED that you never know how you will react in an emergency until you experience one. One afternoon I had just returned to my cabin after playing deck tennis with one of my colleagues and was relaxing on my bed dressed only in a pair of shorts when the alarm bell sounded. This meant every one down to their emergency station in the engine room. After putting on my engine room shoes, I made my way down to the main switchboard flat situated above the generator flat which in turn was above the engine room floor level. The heat on the switchboard flat was intense. This was because one of the turbine generator's main high pressure steam pipes had burst and the superheated steam was escaping and rising onto the switchboard flat. My job was to see that everything on the switchboard was operating satisfactorily and stay there until the emergency was over. After checking that all was in working order, I suddenly became aware that the temperature was rising and that my bare arms and legs were starting to feel uncomfortable to say the least. The air was hot and I needed cool air to breathe so I stood beneath a supply ventilation fan outlet as close as I could get my mouth but the air from the vent was also hot. By this time I was starting to realise that there was no chance of escaping from that flat back up to the entrance of the engine room. The only way out was to descend two flights of metal steps onto the engine room floor kevel and the handrails of those steps would be very hot from the superheated steam. I knew I could not stay where I was otherwise I would collapse with heat exhaustion. I had to get down below. How do I do this without some protection for my hands? After what seemed an eternity, as I was now just about collapsing with exhaustion, I found a piece of cloth behind the switchboard which I tore in half and wrapped round each hand. I then literally staggered back to the stairs, took hold of the rails in each hand and slid down to the engine room floor level without touching the steps. After a drink of water I was taken out of the engine room by another route to the hospital bay where I was examined by the doctor to see if I had suffered any burns. Apart from a few red blotches on my body and mild burns on my hands, I had got off lightly.

I will never forget that experience. It was as near to being caught in a fire though the strange thing was at no time did I panic, I was alert to the situation I was in at all times and I am sure the prayer I said at the time helped. As I said before, you can never foresee how you will react to an emergency. I learned later that one of the engineers had volunteered to go onto the generator flat (with a wet towel covering his head) and close the valve on the turbine which shut off the superheated steam. It only took him a minute to complete the operation but due to the excessive temperature around the generator, he collapsed on his return. Fortunately he soon recovered.

36. The Wedding

O N MY LAST TRIP on board the Carthage a few days out from our home port at King George V Docks, the engineering staff held a party for me and presented me with a box of steak knives and forks as a wedding present. An unexpected though pleasant surprise. This gift is still in use in our house today, although they are only brought out on special occasions.

After four happy trips on the Carthage with Harry and Mike, I left the ship to take a long leave and get married. Mike was to be best man and Harry groomsman but unfortunately Harry never made it to the wedding. He was recalled by the company and instructed to join a cargo ship which sailed just before the happy event.

Mike came up to Newcastle two days before the wedding which gave me an opportunity to show him around the city. There was no stag or hen night so untraditionally, Joan, Mike and I went to Tynemouth and had dinner together in the Grand Hotel. I can remember we enjoyed an excellent meal during which we were serenaded by a Mexican singer playing a guitar, or so I thought. After serenading us with quite a few numbers Mike waved him over to compensate him for his efforts. At this point Joan, in all innocence, asked him what part of Mexico he was from. "Am from Long Benton just up the road pet", was his reply. Joan's face went bright red while Mike and I could not contain our laughter. Well I suppose there's nothing wrong with a 'Geordie Mexican' for as that famous Tyneside song quotes, "Where ever ye gan yer sure to find a 'Geordie'!"

The wedding, on 7 June 1958 went smoothly. The whole day was organised totally by Joan and her mother as I was away at sea. The bride and bridesmaids looked radiant and the groom and best man very smart in their Merchant Navy uniform. The reception went well until Mike had to reply on behalf of the bridesmaids. He stood up ready to speak when he just lost his nerve and couldn't remember what to say. I had to prompt him the whole speech. It was like the ventriloquist and his dummy for I was trying to tell him what to say without moving my lips so no-one would notice! That's the first time I had ever seen Mike beat for words.

After the reception Joan and I left to catch a plane to Jersey in the Channel Isles where we spent one evening before flying over to Guernsey the following day to spend two weeks honeymoon.

37. Sabotage at Sea

On 18 JULY 1958, I reluctantly reported back to King George V Docks where I joined my next ship, the Corfu, which was a sister to my previous ship. She was a 14,293 gross tons passenger liner built by Alexander Stephen & Sons in Glasgow in 1931. Her engines comprised of Parson's single reduction geared steam turbines. Two screws propelled her at a cruising speed of 18 knots. There were 279 crew and she could accommodate 177 first class and 214 second class passengers.

The first trip out on a new vessel, one always felt a little apprehensive as to what the new officers would be like and in particular the chief electrical engineer. This was not a very happy time for me, since I'd only just been married for two and a half months and here was I setting off on another ten week voyage - a long time to be away from your wife. After a while I settled down and made new friends and got on reasonably well with the chief who was one of the most senior officers in the company. The trip went well on the outward voyage to Hong Kong with nothing unusual happening. It was different on the homeward voyage, for the chief electrical engineer started to accuse his staff (me and the third electrical officer) of sabotaging electrical equipment which had been officially reported as needing attention. I had a hard time convincing him that no one was sabotaging the equipment but to no avail for, while he believed that it wasn't his staff, he thought it must be the passengers or the engineering staff.

I diplomatically tried to get him to see the doctor but he wouldn't hear of it. I don't mind saying I was worried about him for you could have a sensible conversation with him most of the time then he would suddenly raise his voice and state that everybody was against him and trying to sabotage the ship's electrical equipment. I did eventually report what was happening to the second engineer who advised me to keep an eye on him to see if things got worse. A week later I had just finished my evening meal and was enjoying coffee with colleagues when I was summoned to the chief electrical engineer's cabin. When I got there he grabbed my arm and took me straight down the engine room to the generator platform and pointed to one of three generators which was not in operation. He shouted "Look there's evidence the machine has been sabotaged!" I looked at the generator and found that the commutator segments had lifted out of position and had broken all the brushes, hence the machine had been stopped and the spare generator started by one of the engineers. Apparently when the generator brushes had started to disintegrate, the alarm had been sounded and the chief had gone down to see what was wrong as he was on cabin watch. When he saw the generator he went berserk, accusing the duty engineer of hitting the generator commutator with a hammer. This was the last straw, the second engineer ordered him to see the doctor who advised that he should stay in the hospital ward until we got back to London. In the meantime I was to take over his duties as chief electrical engineer. Strange how I was promoted twice through unusual circumstances.

38. The Final Voyage

MY FINAL VOYAGE out to Hong Kong and back passed quicker than I expected, probably due to the fact that I managed to get ashore in all the homeward ports giving me the opportunity to visit those places I had missed. It also gave me the chance to add to my collection of photographic slides of all the places I had visited. After many fond farewells from my colleagues, I left the Corfu and resigned from P. & O. on 16 March 1959.

This meant that I had served almost three and a half years with the P.& O. Company. On reflection, I do not think I would have ended my career at sea if I had not got married, for life on board a P.& O. liner was good. The pay was good, the food was good, the female company was good and the opportunity to visit and see places all over the world was something not to be missed. Having said that it was not the career for a married man being away from his wife best part of ten months of each year. Now that I was married, I found it hard to return to my ship after each leave.

There was some consolation in those days in the fact that I was allowed to have my wife on board for the overnight sailing from King George V Docks round to Southampton Docks which had become our new passenger embarkation terminal. Had I volunteered for cargo ship duties then Joan would have been allowed to accompany me on board while the ship visited the European coastal ports. These coastal trips could last quite a few weeks which would have given Joan the chance to visit and see some of the European ports. However I preferred to sacrifice this privilege to stay on the passenger liners.

Looking back at those years spent at sea I realise how fortunate I was to have spent my National service in the Merchant Navy even though it was twice as long a period as I would have had to do in any one of the armed services. I thoroughly enjoyed the three and a half happy years at sea in the Merchant Navy. An experience that not only enhanced my career but also gave me the opportunity to see parts of the world I would never have expected to see and, of course, make many new friends.

39. Back to the Drawing Board

In April 1959, after using up the leave I was due I returned to Vickers naval yard to continue my career as an electrical draughtsman. It took quite a few weeks for me to settle down to drawing office routine after my adventures at sea, however the big consolation was that I was at home every night with my new bride, Joan.

Nothing had changed in the office, the same characters and the same routines were still in operation and there was plenty of work to do. I soon got into the drawing office routine and began enjoying the work, particularly as I was given jobs to do on my own.

One of the most satisfying projects I recall was when I was made a section leader on a contract to build a liner named the Northern Star for the Shaw Saville company. This ship was a passenger liner of about 20,000 tons which normally sailed a scheduled route from Southampton to New Zealand and back. She was launched by the Queen Mother in 1960 and left the yard two years later.

One of the senior section leaders and I were responsible for electrical drawings and ordering of equipment as well as overseeing the progress of the electrical installation on board the vessel. This was all very high pressure work but I loved it.

Throughout my career, I have always enjoyed the job when there was extra pressure put on me. I hated quiet spells when there was little work to do. The pressure was certainly on with this contract for we had to meet a tight work schedule and deadline finishing date. This made it all the more exciting for me even though there were lots of problems to sort out as the ship neared the completion date.

The crowning glory for me was being invited to go on sea trials, a first for me. The sea trials were to last about five days. Sea trials are to prove not only to the owner's representatives but also to shipyard management and personnel that the ship meets all required standards and performs in accordance with the requirements laid down in the contract specification.

Being my first sea trials, I was quite excited and as I was not due on watch until later in the evening, I went up on deck to admire the view as we sailed down the river Tyne. We were ably supported and guided down the river by four tugs, two forward and two aft. Everything was going quite smoothly until we reached the end of the river. However, as we were about to pass the north and south piers, a strong wind blowing from the south caught hold of the ship broadside on and started pushing her towards the north pier.

Panic stations as we got nearer and nearer to the pier and I was convinced nothing would stop us colliding with it. At the last minute the tugs managed to bring the vessel under control and by a mere couple of feet, we sailed past the pier out into the open sea. What a start to the trials - we could hardly believe that we had avoided a serious collision which would not only have seriously damaged the ship but would have also damaged part of the pier wall with devastating costs to the shipyard. Mind you, I think the tug operators would have had to share some of the responsibility along with the pilot navigating the vessel. Anyway it turned out all right in the end.

Being part of company staff, my colleagues and I were allowed to dine in the main passenger dining saloon along with shipyard directors, management and the owner's representatives. The evening dinner was something to remember, for as the owner of the Shaw Saville company was attending the trials and it happened to be his birthday that day, a very special seven course meal was provided with wine to complement each course. This was followed by birthday cake and champagne to toast the chairman. A perfect banquet fit for the occasion. By the time the dinner had finished it was time for my duty watch which comprised recording all electrical power readings of the main generators and auxiliary machinery. It was a long watch as by this time the alcohol was taking effect and all I wanted was my bed!

The following day we did our measured mile trials just off the Northumberland coast then headed north passing the Firth of Forth. It was while we were journeying up the east Scottish coast that Tom Cole, (a colleague of mine), and I decided to try the open-air swimming pool, which by this time had been filled for the use of anyone not on trial duty. There was no one in the pool as Tom and I approached. We stood quite some considerable time just looking at the water. Eventually we decided it would be better to jump in and get used to the water rather than sheepishly test it with our big toes.

In we went. I came up to the surface panting for breath, not because I had gone deep into the water but I was so cold. Tom was standing with his feet on the bottom of the pool and his head just above the water trying to say something to me but could not get the words out for his teeth chattering. We stayed in long enough for a colleague to take our photograph then we got out as fast as we could as by this time we were blue with the cold. I have swam in the North Sea at Tynemouth and at Spittal beach close to Berwick on Tweed many a time when it was cold but nothing as cold as this swimming pool water. It took a few cups of tea and a good rub down to get our circulation back to normal. We found out later that they had filled the pool with sea-water straight out of the North Sea. No wonder it was cold. We had expected it to be heated! Word soon got round the ship and no one attempted to use the pool after that. Despite the cold, Tom and I had the honour of christening the pool.

The following day the ship rounded the top of Scotland where we found the sea was reasonably calm for that time of year. Apart from carrying out our duties, the rest of the time was spent admiring the beautiful Scottish coastal scenery and eating and drinking.

If not on duty in the evening then time was spent after dinner meeting up with some of our electrical foremen and charge-men for drinks in one of the many bars on the ship. All drinks were free on the ship but you had to sign a chitty for whatever you ordered to prevent you from over-indulging. It did not make any difference to our group for we always forged the signature of the ship's electrical manager who was not very happy when at the end of the trials he was asked to account for the excessive number of drinks he had signed for. When he realised what had happened, he just smiled and called us some name which I believe, meant that our mothers were not married.

After five days of successful sea trials we eventually arrived at the mouth of the Clyde where most of us disembarked and set off for home. For most, sea trials were one of the perks of the job for, as some would have it, it enabled you to get away from the wife for a few days and also the money was extremely good.

40. 'Dreadnought'

In THE EARLY SIXTIES, four of us in the electrical drawing office were sent over to Vickers shipyard at Barrow-in-Furness to assist their electrical department in the commissioning of the first British nuclear submarine built in the UK. The four of us, that is, George Hume, George Fenwick, Tom Cole and I reported to the shipyard gate where we were admitted and directed to an office alongside where the nuclear sub was being fitted out.

The security guard at the office was curious to know how we had managed to get so far through the building without a security pass and here we were looking out onto Britain's top secret submarine. Talk about terrorists. Anyway the laughable part about it was that we could not leave the building until we had all the correct passes needed. It was easy to get into the place but a darned sight harder to leave!

Our first task after meeting the department head was to sort out our lodgings. We had two addresses given to us so we split into pairs, the two older Georges would share one accommodation and the younger Tom and I the other. Both houses were on a small strip of land called Walney Island which was joined to the mainland by a bridge.

Tom and I stayed in a very neat and tidy house occupied by the landlady, who was named Maud, her husband Jim and their teenage son, whose name was also Jim. Tom and I slept in a huge bedroom with two single beds each with cotton sheets and blankets. I mention this because we arrived there in the middle of January and while there was a nice big fire always burning in the living room, there was no central heating in the house so the bedroom was very cold. Can you imagine jumping into bed between two freezing cold cotton sheets and trying to sleep? Eventually I did pluck up enough courage to ask if we could each have a hot water bottle (which I don't normally approve of as I like to warm up naturally) but oh those sheets, I'll never forget them!

Barring those sheets, everything was perfect. We were made most welcome and the food was plain but wholesome with generous helpings of it. Nothing was a trouble to Maud and she could not do enough for Tom and me. Her husband was a bus driver and very proud of it. His general conversation was always about buses and how if ever there was a nuclear accident on the submarine then once the warning siren had sounded he was responsible for organising the buses to evacuate the residents in the town, a most important job according to Jim.

The two Georges, Tom and I were assigned to carry out testing on certain parts of the electrical systems but not the nuclear control circuits which were covered by their own personnel. As we were sworn to secrecy on the projects we were involved with I can't really say much other than to reflect on some of the light hearted events which took place while we were there.

George Hume (the one that got stuck in the torpedo tube) was given the task of testing out circuits on one of the auxiliary control panels. Unfortunately for George a fault indicating light appeared on the control panel one day and as much as he tried he could not find the fault so the alarm indicating light remained on. Now as it happened this panel was situated just below the conning tower where everyone who came on board had to pass it. Each morning and evening the Ministry of Defence overseers would pass by George and sarcastically say to him, "I see you still haven't got the light to go out yet." In other words you have not found the fault. This went on for weeks as by this time George was testing other parts of the panel and leaving the faulty circuit alone. This continuous sarcasm however got on George's nerves and he decided he was going to solve the fault and extinguish the indicating light once and for all. The next day I boarded the vessel and stood chatting with my colleagues in the control room when one of the overseers shouted to George, much to our surprise for we had not noticed, "I see you've got rid of the alarm light at last, how did you get rid of the fault?" George, quick as a flash, replied "I removed the indicating lamp!" The overseer's face was a picture of astonishment but when it had sunk in he saw the funny side as indeed we all did and each of the following overseers was given the same reply. Before the vessel was completed George did solve the problem but was never allowed to forget that when all is lost, remove the lamp!

I was amazed at the room inside a nuclear sub, very much bigger than a conventional sub, although it was impossible to walk upright in some areas. One night the four of us were working overtime and the sub was fairly quiet with few personnel on board. As usual there was a problem so we thought, well, four heads are better than one. To get to the fuse box where the problem was, we had to descend a short wooden ladder into a compartment where the head room was only about five feet and the box was positioned in the opposite corner to the only entrance. There was no deck plating down so we had to pick our way precariously across pipes and steel beams to our destination. It was while we were all standing facing this fuse box contemplating what the fault could be when I suddenly stepped back to ease my aching body as I was standing like a hunchback and unknowingly stepped onto a lever which opened a high pressure air valve. The noise was horrendous in such a small compartment. None of us knew what was happening at first but after those few brief seconds, the other three had scampered back and up the ladder led by 'Torpedo George' who was the smallest, while I was still standing there covering my ears to deaden the noise. After what seemed an eternity I looked down and saw what I had done then quickly bent down and shut the valve. When I caught up with my colleagues, their excuse for a speedy exit was that they thought there had been an explosion so the best solution was run. I asked "What about me left down there hardly able to move?" As quickly as they could their reply was, "We would have called the fire brigade to come and rescue you." Some friends and colleagues, I have to admit. We smiled about it but at the time it was no laughing matter.

One of the test procedures, as the vessel neared completion, was to blow the tanks. These tanks are fitted along each side of the vessel and are filled to enable the submarine to sink and when resurfacing air is blown into the tanks forcing the water out thus enabling the vessel to resurface. On this occasion the tanks had been partially filled with water ready for the blow operation. I and a few others who were working in the galley, which was right below one of the escape hatches two decks down, did not know that this test was about to take place. For this test the vessel is well secured to the jetty as when the tanks are blown the water forced out creates a huge wave between the jetty and the submarine. The test began and suddenly water started to pour down the opening from the conning tower to the galley. The next thing I heard someone shout "We're sinking!". This time I did not wait to evaluate the situation, I was off like a shot, first up the ladder and straight up out of the escape hatch and onto the deck where the water was now receding. Fortunately a false alarm but what had happened was when they blew the tanks, the force of water between the vessel and the jetty had been so great that it had overflowed onto the deck and entered the escape hatches. Amusing for those doing the test in the control room seeing the sub being abandoned by all these figures rushing up the ladders to escape but not so amusing for us who knew nothing about the test. It would have made a great Lowry painting!

Our landlady, Maud, was not always at home when Tom and I arrived after working overtime. She would be out at the local cinema enjoying her favourite pastime, Bingo, but our dinner would always be there for us, either in the oven or on top of a pan of boiling water. One night when we were not working overtime, Maud would insist that we accompany her to the Bingo hall. I vaguely remember buying tickets but spent the rest of the evening amused by the expression on the faces of those playing as they concentrated on marking the numbers on their cards. One winner happened to be up in the circle and so a little cloth bag tied to a piece of string was lowered over the circle balcony for the winnings to be put in and hauled back up to be presented to the winner. Tom and I had to laugh but overall we were quite bored with it all. Of course we did not let on to Maud.

Saturday afternoon was Maud's shopping day in Barrow-in-Furness. She had not left the house a minute this particular Saturday when she came rushing back in saying she had forgotten her board which she needed as she was buying herself a new handbag. It was not until she returned that we found out why she needed a small plastic board before she could buy her new handbag. It was her Bingo board which she used to clip her Bingo tickets to. She needed the board with her to make sure it would fit into the new handbag. What can you say, it was her hobby.

Every three weeks we were allowed to go home for the weekend. This was a long journey of anywhere up to six hours which meant we never got home until Friday evening but it was worth it, for now I had a daughter, Judith, to see as well as my wife Joan. It was all too short a stay though for I had to set off back to Barrow after lunch on Sunday as the train connections were hopeless. I would eventually arrive back in Barrow on the milk train from Lancaster at about six am which did not give me much time for sleep before reporting into work.

One weekend Tom brought his car back to Barrow so the next leave he invited me to go with him in the car, sharing the petrol cost. The quickest route was the road over Shap which is normally a pleasant run in summer but bearing in mind that this was the middle of February we took a risk. The weather was fine when we left Barrow but as we got into the Lakes and started to climb up the mountain roads it began to snow. By the time we got to the top of Shap it was blowing a blizzard. To make matters worse the car windscreen wipers stopped working. Fortunately the car, an old Wolseley, had wipers you could operate by hand which meant turning a lever on the dashboard from the horizontal position left through ninety degrees right. From the top of Shap I was sat leaning forward turning this windscreen lever back and forth with my right hand, no gloves on, no heating in the car, all of fifty miles home to Newcastle. My hand was frozen and my back and wrist ached for days after. Needless to say Tom never took the car back to Barrow. I'll never forget that journey, it was horrendous. How we stayed on the road was beyond me, we were lucky to escape a serious accident. When you're young you learn your lessons the hard way.

Our work at Barrow was now completed although the submarine would not be ready for sea trials for another few weeks. It would have been nice to have been involved in the final commissioning and possible sea trials although on second thoughts I've never fancied going underwater. The six months that we were there was mainly hard work for we worked six days and at least four nights per week with very little social life. Overall though, we enjoyed the experience, made plenty of money and had some good laughs. Now it was back to the grind at the Naval Yard.

Not long after returning from Barrow I was invited to work in the estimating section under Tom who had been promoted to electrical estimating manager. This was completely different work to being a draughtsman. It was all about figures, costing materials and labour and negotiating with sub-contractor representatives. Once I got into the job I found it very satisfying, particularly when the company won an order from the overall estimate submitted to the owners. By this time the office was beginning to modernise; out went slide-rules, log tables and mechanical number recording machines and in came the electronic calculator. The first few days using the calculator were treated with apprehension for I was checking all calculator answers to make sure it was correct. Eventually I accepted the electronic device and had to admit it did speed up calculations tremendously.

41. The Consortium

LIFE AT THIS STAGE was pretty good for I was earning good money to help towards paying the mortgage on a three bedroom house we had bought in High Heaton, a suburb of Newcastle. Also I now had two lovely daughters, Judith and Jill, and Joan my wife to look after. I was even contemplating buying my first car, a second hand Morris Oxford.

In 1966 just when things seemed to be going along nicely at work the directors dropped a bomb by announcing that the four largest yards on the Tyne were to merge and form a consortium. The consortium was to comprise Vickers naval yard, Swan Hunters yard, Hawthorne Leslie's yard and Redhead's yard. The merger had been mooted for some time, the biggest problem being where the headquarters should be.

The Naval Yard was the obvious choice as it was the largest of all the yards and the launching facilities were ideal, particularly for the larger vessels. It was thought that perhaps ships should be built in a more modern style by having a covered dock to erect them in. This could have been adapted easily at the Naval Yard where there was plenty of space. However, Swans, being the largest shareholder, insisted the head office and works should be sited at Wallsend. The announcement created all sorts of fears and rumours throughout the Tyne yards. Were there going to be redundancies, change of work place, closing down of some yards? Fears and speculation were the only topics of conversation at that time.

Being partly owned by Vickers Barrow, some of the technical staff at the

Naval Yard were given the opportunity of applying for similar positions at the Barrow yard. I discussed the offer with Joan but I had already made up my mind that I would not like to live in Barrow having already sampled the area whilst lodging. There was nothing particularly wrong with Barrow town or the surrounding area, for the beautiful Lake District is close at hand but there's only one way in and out of Barrow. It's a dead end and the whole community's main topic of conversation centres around Vickers shipyard and engineering works. Although Joan had not been to Barrow she needed no persuading to stay put, hence I did not apply and decided to stay with the consortium come what may. A few weeks after the consortium announcement I was invited to attend an interview with the electrical estimating and contracts manager at the Swan Hunter's Wallsend yard. There I met the manager, a gentleman named Joe Lavery, who after half an hour's interview offered me the position of electrical estimator.

Joe was a clever electrical engineer, one of the best in the company. He had a great influence on my future career for which I was very grateful. It did not take long to adapt to the Swan's way of doing things. Joe's department comprised six estimators, one clerk and a typist. Over the years, personnel changed amongst some of the younger staff but I will never forget two of the older estimators. Harry Holstead sat next to me at work. He too had been transferred from another yard, namely Hawthorne Leslie, on the opposite side of the river. Harry like me was a Methodist and greatly involved in Church affairs. He and I became great friends over the years. He was a true gentleman in every sense of the word, a quiet and unassuming person who never spoke ill of anyone and his wife had the same qualities, a perfect couple.

Opposite to me sat Birkett McCardle who also became a good friend. Birket not only worked for Joe but also R.I. Smith (known by the staff as 'Smithy') who was the electrical director. Birket was good at his job, was very outspoken and honest. Birket had two main dislikes. First, even though he was never in the armed forces, he hated all Germans. Every German to him was a Nazi. Even years after the war had ended no one could convince him otherwise.

The second dislike was holidays. He always reckoned that they were unsettling and upset the body's normal routine. I can understand that philosophy as I get older, particularly if one is travelling abroad. There is the hassle of waiting at airports, delayed flights, too hot a temperature at your chosen resort and of course eating and drinking far more than normal.

Birket had two bad habits, one was clearing the wax out of each ear every afternoon with a ladies hair grip and the other was smoking. How on earth he did not damage his eardrums is beyond explanation, for this was a daily routine. They talk about passive smoking these days, I must have been a passive smoker for several years for the smoke from Birket's cigarettes always drifted across the two desks into my face. I suffered this for many years sometimes with pretentious coughing and sneezing in the hope he would cease but to no avail and I was very reluctant to object to it at the time. It was not until after he retired that the company eventually banned smoking in the offices.

42. Launches

During the building of any ship there are three special occasions. The first being the laying of the keel, the second the launch and the third its departure from the yard. The keel laying was generally a small private ceremony with owners and company directors. The departure was a sad occasion particularly if you had worked on a ship from start to finish, for you became attached to it. It was like saying farewell to a brother or sister who was leaving home. The occasion I liked best was the launch of the ship, particularly if there was royalty present as then you had the public as well as the special guests invited.

The launch ceremony never ceased to excite me over the many years I witnessed them. It was always a colourful and happy occasion with families and friends of the workers waiving their flags and cheering as royalty appeared. Then a tremendous cheer would erupt as the champagne bottle broke on the bow and that mighty mass of steel would start to slowly move and gracefully glide down the launch ways into the river. There, two or three tugs would be waiting to gently guide her into position for photographs then finally nudge her into her fitting out berth position.

One little piece of information that not many people know about, outside or inside the yard come to think of it, is that the launch champagne bottle is prepared by the Head Tracer. She scribes the bottle with a glass cutter so that it easily breaks when it hits the bow of the ship. The bottle is then decorated with ribbons, the colours of which are selected to suit the owner's company colours or in red white and blue for a naval ship. Even with the bottle scribed I have seen many launches where the bottle has refused to break the first, second and even third time of striking the bow. If it does not move then hydraulic jacks push against the bow giving it just enough momentum to start it gliding down the ways. The bottle refusing to break the first time and the ship refusing to move immediately all adds to the excitement of a launch day.

Not everybody is happy at the start of a launch. The architect responsible for calculating the angle the ship is to be built on the ways and the speed it should travel down them usually looks very apprehensive, wondering if his calculations are correct, but then all goes well and its congratulations all round for achieving another perfect launch.

On a launch day I used to go along to the launch ways and stand beneath the ship at the bow and look down the length of the underside of the vessel. By this time the ship was almost ready to be launched with almost all the support chocks knocked out and the ship resting on the ways held back by a mechanical launching trigger lever and a few remaining chocks. What a marvellous experience to see that vast expanse of steel just above my head extending down the ways to the river's edge.

One of the most historical features about the Swan Hunter yard was that the Roman Wall, which ran from Carlisle to Wallsend, actually terminated in Swan's yard at the head of No.1 berth. Now when it was decided to build the 'big tankers', as they were known, they found that the ways were not long enough to accommodate them so they had to extend the ways considerably. In order to do this, they had to move the Roman Wall back a considerable distance into the bank side to allow for the ways and space for a launching platform as well as room for transport to get past. It proved to be quite a large and expensive operation but there was a lot of money to be made in building these large vessels. Above the bank-side where the wall ended there was a railway line that ran from the yard to the main local British Rail line, as it was then known. Beyond this line was a stone wall which was part of the boundary of the yard. On the other side of this wall were streets of terraced houses the ends of which faced the wall. I mention this detail as when one of the big tankers was fully erected on the ways the bows used to extend over the railway line and boundary wall just up to the end of one of the terraced streets. So when you walked down that particular street all you saw was the huge bow of the ship towering over the end of the street.

Launches were special occasions for the shipyard and the ship owners. Particularly for those who had an invitation to the launching ceremony. One of the most exciting launches to witness was the 250,000 ton tankers which were built at the Swan Hunter yard. There was a great party atmosphere on these occasions for it was also an opportunity for the shipyard workers and staff families to attend.

At each launch the ship had tied to it several sets of drag chains placed at each side of the ways to slow the vessel down as she glided down the ways into the water. To hear the noise and see the movement of these chains as the ship entered the water was always an exciting experience for me. The dust created from these chains was quite prolific. One launch day, the wind blew from the river straight up the launch ways and onto the launching platform. Once the ship had been launched and the drag chains came into operation the dust was blown onto the launch platform where all the dignitaries were assembled in their Sunday best. All you could see was this great rusty cloud of dust enveloping the dignitaries. This caused great confusion amongst them to the utter delight of the families gathered around the platform who then raised a sarcastic cheer at the dignitaries' embarrassment.

The launch of a ship is a wonderful sight to behold and I never tired of witnessing such an event. A launch is the act of sending the completed hull of a new vessel from its position of construction into the water. The hull of a ship is supported on keel blocks while she is being built and held in position by stout wooden timbers generally known as 'shores'. When the hull is completed, the dead-weight is gradually edged from the keel blocks to wooden cradles or sliding 'ways', which rest on launching ways which lead down into the river. In the case of very large ships, a softwood cushion is fitted under the cradle supporting the bow to soften the great load concentrated there at one point during the launch, when the vessel's aft end is supported by the water and the forward end is still on the ways. When the hull is ready to be launched, the launching ways are covered with thick grease, the keel blocks are removed and the weight of the ship is taken wholly on the cradles being held stationary by mechanical triggers. The wooden shores holding her steady are then knocked away and the hull is ready for launching.

In the case of very large ships, such as the quarter million ton tankers, a hydraulic ram is erected each side of the bow to start the hull moving down the ways if it does not go immediately the triggers are released. Heavy drag chains are attached to both sides of the hull to slow it down and bring it to a stop when fully water-borne. The two major concerns with respect to a launch are the tide and the wind. Ships are launched according to the state of the tide and the time of launching has to be adjusted to the moment when the tide is exactly right. If it is launched when the tide is too low then there is a tendency for the stern to droop before it is supported by the river water. If too high then hull distortion may occur when the stern gets waterborne with the weight of the remainder of the hull still taken on the ways.

Ships are always launched stern first so that the rudder and propellers are not damaged by the drag chains as the hull enters the water. If, on the day of the launch, the wind is above a certain velocity then the directors have to make the decision whether to postpone the launch and just have a naming ceremony or take a risk in the hope that the tugs will be able to cope with the vessel in the strong wind once launched.

Royalty paid a small but important part in the life of the shipyard, for the presence of a Royal guest on the day of any launch was always an added attraction to those attending. I must say that there was always something special about a launch, particularly a Royal one, for there was always an air of excitement and expectation. The excitement would build up as the visitors entered the yard for the first time and witnessed this mammoth steel structure lying gracefully on its launch ways, ready to be launched, most of them wondering how such a mass of steel could move down the ways into the river and stay afloat. Then, the expectation of finding a good viewing spot, not only to see the actual launch but also to see the Royal visitor or dignitary performing the ceremony, followed by the yard directors and owners accompanied by their wives and the rest of the launch platform guests. A warm sunny day to enhance the occasion was a bonus to making launches such a special event in the life of the shipyard and all those privileged to attend. Most would acknowledge that it was, for them, a great occasion in their lives.

I attended four Royal launches in my career, three as a spectator and one as an invited guest. The first three launches were performed by H.R.H. Princess Margaret, Princess Anne and the Queen Mother respectively and the fourth by H.M. the Queen.

A few weeks prior to the day of a Royal launch all hell would be let loose with respect to preparing the yard and surrounding areas for the big day. The launch platform would be erected and decorated with red, white and blue bunting, sunken railway tracks temporally filled in where Royalty would walk. All buildings within eyesight would be repainted and flower tubs strategically placed to enhance the appearance of the entrance into the yard premises. Money spent on smartening up the yard and entrance for a Royal visit seemed excessive, nevertheless on the day of the launch the whole place looked special for the Royal guest.

Apart from all the decorative preparation there was the security aspect to consider. This would entail security personnel checking the yard and offices for explosive devices and the presence of the police to control the crowd on the day of the launch. There was one occasion when H.M. the Queen Mother was invited to launch a Naval ship and prior to the launch, which was to take place in the afternoon, the security police came round the offices with a sniffer dog to make sure that there were no explosive devices hidden anywhere. The staff had either gone down the yard to witness the launch or had gone home, so there was only the chief draughtsman and me left in the drawing office.

Now there was one electrical manager who was a bit of a boffin and was used by the company to solve all technical and design problems as well as doing repairs to faulty equipment. His office comprised of the usual desk and chair with a bench around two sides of the office walls. Now Jim's office was unique in that every conceivable bit of space was covered with papers, plans, magazines and pieces of equipment to a depth of about two feet high. He was a most untidy person. One really had to see it to believe the sheer mass of paper and equipment that littered his office desks and floor, so much so that the cleaners would not attempt to clean his office, not that Jim would let them. Despite what I can only describe as this unholy mess, Jim seemed to know where everything was for he always managed to find what he was looking for.

The point of telling you all this is that when the security men came with their dogs to check out Jim's office, they took one look inside, pulled the dogs out and said "No way are we going to attempt to search this office, it looks as though a bomb has already gone off in there!" They then left having been assured that Jim's office did not pose as a security threat.

Almost all work would cease on the day of a Royal Launch. Workmen would be given the option of obtaining a ticket that would admit him and his family to the launch ceremony or he could go home two hours before the ceremony commenced. The yard band would be playing a selection of popular music to keep the crowd entertained up to an hour before the launch ceremony. Ten minutes to launch, all the yard and staff workers and their families would be assembled around the launch platform with a passage-way left for the Royal and special invited guests to make their way from the limousines which had conveyed them from the offices to the launch platform. This was always an exciting time for the ladies assembled; for the platform guests, who were all dressed in their finery, walked in pairs one behind the other up to the platform, preening like peacocks at the "oohs" and "aahs" of the crowd at witnessing such an expensive and elaborate fashion display.

Once on the platform, the National Anthem would be played then a prayer would be given by the local vicar or if Royalty were present, the bishop. Then the chairman of the yard would check the time and if all launching procedures were ready, he would invite the Royal visitor to launch the vessel. The Royal visitor would then take hold of the bottle of champagne and swing it towards the bow of the ship in the hope that it would break. Many is the time it has taken more than two or three swings of the bottle before it would break and each attempt would be greeted with a rapturous cheer from the workers and families. At later launches a more modern system was devised ensuring that the bottle made contact with the ship's bow and broke immediately. This was a chrome metal device which held the bottle horizontal to the platform and the bow of the ship. The bottle was released electrically by a trigger or button by the person launching the ship. Once released, the metal device sprang out towards the bow of the ship making sure the bottle would be broken first time. Once the bottle had christened the ship, there would be a pause of a few seconds before the trigger mechanism holding the ship on the ways came into operation. The ship would slowly start to move down the slip-way slowly gathering speed. Then, as the stern of the ship entered the river, the drag chains fitted either side of the vessel would slow her down, ready for tugs to take over the task of holding her in position at the end of the slip-way while photographs were taken.

All this took place amidst a cheering assembly of very proud and happy people. Once the photographs had been taken the tugs would slowly guide the newly launched vessel alongside one of the berths where she would remain to be fitted out and completed before going out of the river to do her sea trials.

Meanwhile, the launch party would leave the platform and parade back to the limousines where they were driven to a grand reception either at the staff restaurant, a reputable hotel or reception building in the city.

The above events are a brief description of what takes place at a Royal or for that matter any other launch when things went smoothly. However, events did not always go smoothly. At one of the early launches I went to, the lady launching the vessel swung the bottle so hard towards the bow of the ship that most of the champagne sprayed back and soaked those guests at the front of the launch platform much to the delight of the crowd watching below.

Then there was the launch of one of the 250,000 ton tankers at Swan Hunters yard where once the bottle had hit the bow the ship did not move. Every one stood there wondering why she would not move. The design architects were now beginning to look very worried indeed. Then the two hydraulic rams fitted at either side of the bow came into operation trying to push her into motion. The rams at first seemed to have no effect for I saw smoke coming from them as the hydraulics endeavoured to move her. Then, after what seemed like an age, the ship finally moved smoothly down the launch-way into the river.

At the launch of a cargo vessel at the Naval Yard, the ship moved off down the launch–ways into the river but before the tugs could get a hold of her she had gone straight over the other side and knocked down one corner of the local paint factory. The ship had obviously gone down the launch–ways too fast implying that some design architect had gone astray with his calculations.

Launches, as I said before, did not take place if it was too windy, however on one particular day, the management decided to take a risk. The vessel glided down the ways comfortably into the river but as the tugs were about to get their towing lines aboard her, the wind suddenly increased, caught her broadside on and swept her bow into the local ferry jetty which suffered a considerable amount of damage. Eventually the tugs brought the ship under control and managed to move her safely alongside the fitting-out berth where, after a rigorous inspection of the bow, it was found that no damage had been done. Of course, the Port of Tyne Authority would have to be compensated for the damage inflicted to their ferry landing.

As shipbuilding progressed, so more and more fittings were erected on the vessel before launch thereby cutting down on the fitting-out stages of the ship's programme. One ship due to be launched had her funnel fitted and on the day of the launch as she moved down the launch-ways smoke was seen coming out of the funnel, much to the surprise of the spectators. Now many of those attending not conversant with shipbuilding believed the ship was travelling down the ways under her own power but in actual fact some wag had set light to an oily rag and placed it in the funnel just as the ship was launched. It made headlines in the evening edition of the local papers.

To be invited to a launch ceremony was, as far as I was concerned, a privilege, others would disagree. It used to rile me to see young men on the launch platform who had hardly worked in the yard a couple of years but because of their position of being a shop steward they were invited to the launch ceremony. Yet here was I with forty plus years service with the company and never had an invite. It was not so much for myself that I craved an invitation but for Joan, my wife, who I always felt would enjoy such an occasion.

I have to thank my director, Bob Wilson, for my first invitation to the launch of the cable laying vessel named 'Sir Cedric Sharpe' built for the Cable and Wireless company. The ship was launched by the wife of one the company directors. Both Joan and I thoroughly enjoyed the occasion. The second invitation was a little more spectacular, for it was to witness the launch of the Antarctic survey ship 'James Clarke Ross' by her Majesty the Queen and afterwards luncheon with her Majesty at the banqueting hall of the Civic Centre in Newcastle.

The ship was to be named after Sir James Clarke Ross, the most experienced polar explorer of the century, who lived from 1800 to 1862. The launch day was a Saturday and all invited guests were to be at the company offices where canapés and drinks were taken prior to the arrival of the Queen. Joan and I, along with other invited guests, were seated in a specially erected stand for the occasion overlooking the launch platform. The surrounding area of the yard was crowded with spectators many of who were families of some of the workers who had been involved in building the ship. Everyone was out to enjoy themselves for the management had provided flags and balloons for the children and the company silver band played popular tunes for entertainment.

The arrival of the Queen into the yard brought rapturous applause. The applause was acknowledged with her usual wave. After being introduced to some of the company staff she ascended the steps onto the launch platform where, after a blessing of the ship by the clergy, she named the vessel and pressed the button which released the trigger that enabled the ship to glide gracefully down the launch ways. This was the signal for the gathered crowd to cheer the ship on her way. We followed the Royal party from the platform through an aisle of cheering families who had not only come to see the Queen but also the spectacular outfits worn by the invited guests. It was a little embarrassing to say the least, being stared at by hundreds of people although I'm sure Joan enjoyed every minute of it, dressed in her new gold and black striped outfit, enhanced by a large brimmed black hat, with a beautiful tan coloured feather attached. My shoulders shot back and my chest stuck out a little more as we passed through the crowd and I detected a voice directed at Joan saying "By Hinny, she looks as smart as the Queen!"

Four coaches took the invited guests to the civic centre. The whole journey was controlled by the police who had motorcycle outriders escorting the coaches and stopping traffic at all the road junctions. We all felt like royalty. For most of the route, people stood waving and smiling.

The banquet was excellent, just as you would expect on a royal visit. As a company representative, I was host to eleven guests seated at my table with a good view of the royal table. Most of my guests were staff of the Antarctic survey team that had spent time surveying and recording scientific projects carried out in the Antarctic. Their intriguing stories proved to be exciting and amusing and filled in the time up to the royal and company toasts. Toasts were then followed by a wonderful display of marching and music by the Royal Marines Band from Portsmouth. This was certainly a highlight for the guests, seeing the band marching back and forth between the tables, playing all the popular marches with the music reverberating around the huge hall to the timely clapping of the audience. An event never to be forgotten by all who attended. At long last after forty years service I had been invited to a company launch, would you believe it, two in the same year. As Joan reminded me it was worth waiting for.

43. Management

A FEW YEARS LATER there was a restructuring within the electrical department and Joe, my boss, was promoted to electrical general manager which meant his old job was vacant. There were two of us who applied for the position and I was accepted. I recall saying to Harry and Birket many a time in the past that I would not like Joe's job, yet here I was in my own office having been appointed electrical estimating and contracts manager. The promotion and increase in salary were very welcome.

As a manager covering estimating, contracts, initial design and writing specifications, it gave me the opportunity to represent the department on many occasions and to meet and discuss prospective and contractual orders with owners not only from this country but abroad. These trips were always welcome, for apart from getting out of the office, it was an opportunity to enjoy the company of fellow managers and directors and also meet other companies' personnel.

Travelling abroad was always a pleasure as the company allowed business class travel and first class accommodation. There were many company visits to the Ministry of Defence offices at Fox-Hill in the city of Bath. It was here on one particular visit that I had to give my first presentation of a proposed electrical design for a Ministry of Defence vessel the company were tendering for. There were about eight of our company representatives sat on one side of a very long table and approximately thirty Ministry representatives on the other side which was daunting to say the least. My presentation was the last one on the agenda so while sitting through the hull and engineering ones, the tension slowly built up inside me and by the time I was called upon to give the electrical presentation my stomach was churning and I was sweating profusely. I stood up, mouth absolutely dry, facing thirty seven pairs of staring eyes all glued in my direction. I took advantage of having a drink of water before commencing, just giving enough time to compose myself.

After all the worry and anxiety the presentation went well and it was a great relief to find that there were no awkward questions to follow. After this presentation, all others would be a doddle!

A presentation given to the naval personnel in Lagos, Nigeria, has to be the most embarrassing experience of all technical presentations I gave on behalf of the company. There were four of us selected to go to Nigeria, the contracts director, the naval architect, the engineering general manager and myself. A week before we were due to leave, Bob Goudy the engineering general manager and I had to fill in some forms in order to get our visas. Bob decided that we should fill in the forms together to make sure they were both filled in correctly. One of the questions was "Have you been abroad recently?" Bob told me he could not remember. I burst out laughing, to Bob's annoyance, until I reminded him that he had been on a memory course the previous day! Having said that, I puzzled over the same question, trying hard to remember when I had last been abroad. Bob got his own back by reminding me that I had been in Holland, two days ago. I really did not think the Holland trip should have counted for I was there and back in one day and my business was all carried out in one of the airport's private conference rooms, still I have to agree it was on foreign soil. They say memory plays tricks with every individual at some time in life, to Bob and me it just seemed to be a little too early.

44. Nigeria

WHEN THE PARTY LEFT FOR LAGOS, Nigeria the following week, on arrival at Heathrow Airport, our director made a bee-line for the duty free shop and filled a trolley with a mixture of bottles of spirits and cigars. Each of us in our party was instructed by our director to take four of these bottles of spirits each with a box of cigars through the Nigerian customs when we arrived. These were gifts for the company agent who, apart from accepting some himself, would pass them on to senior personnel in the Nigerian naval establishment to whom our design presentation was to be made. I found out later that it was common practice and expected by the hosts in certain countries to be offered gifts before or during negotiating any contract with them. Does this sound like bribery?

During our flight to Lagos, I took advantage of checking up on what passengers were permitted to take into Nigeria and found that all spirits were accepted except brandy. This immediately raised alarm bells as I was the only one carrying brandy in my case. I raised the issue with our director who nonchalantly said everything would be alright and that I would not be stopped by Customs, don't worry about it. The trouble was I could not stop worrying about it. I did not fancy landing up in a Nigerian jail.

Our director was right. The custom's personnel never stopped anyone who had travelled on our aircraft. However a strange thing happened as we were waiting to go through the passport section of customs. We had all handed our passports into the desk marked 'foreign visitors' and were waiting for them to be stamped when a voice over the speaker system requested my immediate presence at the desk. Arriving at the desk, I was told that my passport had to be taken to the Nigerian desk for stamping, much to my surprise, for that was where the arriving Nigerian citizens were getting their passports stamped. Who was I to argue with Nigerian customs official?

The local arrivals desk was seething with Nigerians with no orderly queue and by this time my colleagues had passed on into the airport building. I thought to myself, I could be here all day waiting to get to the counter and being the only white person amongst all these local people pushing and shoving each other there was no way that I was going near them. I did eventually work my way around to the back of the customs desk and managed to attract the attention of one of the officials. He took my passport and stamped it without giving me any explanation as to why I had to go through the Nigerian section of customs. Was it my middle name of Alonzo that sent me to the locals desk? I doubt it very much for the name is of Spanish origin. Why, I will never know and I don't intend going back to find out! Meeting up with my colleagues I was greeted in very poor broken English/Nigerian voices suggesting that I was now one of the locals!

Having safely got through customs, which was a great relief to me, we then had to go to another desk to pay a sum of money for entering the country. What a rip-off I thought although on reflection it would bring quite a bit of money into a country which badly needed it, but then to crown it all, you had to pay to get out again!

The hotel we stayed in was of a reasonably high standard situated on the outskirts of the city of Lagos. The hotel had no doors to the entrance, so anyone could walk in. Our director suggested we all meet by the swimming pool where it would be nice and cool, for by this time it was beginning to get dark. I had taken obviously taken a lot longer than the rest of our party to shower and change, for when I arrived at our agreed meeting spot, everyone was there. As well as our party there were two agents who worked for Swans, plus four young, well-dressed ladies, who I assumed to be the wives or secretaries of the agents.

Light-hearted talk and drinks went down well in the heat of the evening. It was not until the four ladies got up and left the group to go to the toilet that I raised the question to one of the agents as to which one was his wife. The reply was a shock for he said none of them were, they were there for anyone's pleasure, would I like to be introduced to one of them? Apparently these ladies of the night were allowed to come into the hotel any time of the day or night and sell their 'wares' to the male residents. Our agents thought we might like to partake. How wrong he was, for not only were we all happily married men, but this country was rife with Aids. Another little eye-opener on my travels.

The following day was our big event, for we were going to the Nigerian naval offices to present our designs and show a model of the proposed naval vessel we thought they may like to order from us. Our journey there by taxi was not without incident. We got stuck in a line of traffic on a flyover on the motorway and from nowhere, a young Nigerian boy appeared knocking on the window asking if we would like to buy one of his souvenirs that he had balanced on a tray which was tied round his neck. All that was between our taxi and the edge of the flyover was a foot wide concrete parapet and a fifty foot drop down the other side. How this boy managed to get there was beyond comprehension and how was he allowed to do it? You really have to witness these incidents to appreciate how the other half of the world lives.

When we arrived at the office we were greeted by the doorman who insisted we give him a biro pen, then by the desk clerk who also wanted one. We seemed to spend quite a time handing out biros before reaching our destination but this was the custom for any European when visiting any office. I now knew why I was instructed to pack two dozen biros in my case before we set off from home!

The whole day was a disaster, for the naval hierarchy we were supposed to meet did not turn up. We later found out that although he had an appointment to see us he had gone off for a few days holiday. Our director was not very pleased, however we were directed to his deputy's office where we were introduced and where we presented a model of the proposed naval ship design. To our utter amazement the Nigerian naval representative told us to put the model on the desk, thanked us for it, and said goodbye. Our agent was furious and made it clear to the Nigerian that the four representatives from Swan Hunters had not travelled four thousand miles just to hand over a ship model.

After all that some higher rank personnel was summoned who apologised and thereafter a meeting was arranged with the presentation to be delivered the following afternoon. Even this did not go smoothly for during each presentation naval personnel were walking in and out of the room and showing very little interest in what was being delivered about the ship design. In the end we were glad to leave, for they showed us no courtesy and were downright rude in my opinion. Our agent assured us that everything would be fine, the design was good and providing the price was right, then we stood a good chance of getting the order. I was not convinced and felt sure they only wanted our design.

Lagos was not a place I would wish to return to, for it was not clean, it had a serious traffic problem and I never felt safe walking outside the hotel during the day, never mind the evening. One day we had the afternoon off, so Dennis, Bob and I went out for a walk to get some fresh air as the temperature was in the nineties in the hotel grounds. We headed towards the sea where we thought there would be a breeze. We had not gone very far when I was accosted by a young man trying to sell an ivory bracelet. After having no luck with me, he then went on to pester Dennis who finally got rid of him by telling the young man that Bob would love his bracelet. Well, this guy never left Bob alone, he followed him everywhere we went. As we approached the beach, I thought it would be nice to have a photograph of some of the local Nigerian women who were dressed in very colourful outfits. I would be a little discreet and take the photo from a safe distance so as not to embarrass anyone. In the meantime Bob and Dennis had set off running along the beach, hoping to get rid of the bracelet seller who had now become a real menace to Bob who could not convince the chap that he wasn't interested in his wares.

As I got onto the beach the small group of Nigerian ladies, who I had taken a photograph of, were running towards me fists raised and obviously shouting obscenities in their local language. Oh, oh, what do I do now? Trying to explain to them In English that I was not really taking their photo was to no avail as they crowded round me, pointing at the camera. Things did not look too healthy for me as Dennis and Bob, by this time, were out of sight and who should now be walking towards me and the hysterical ladies but a Nigerian policeman. He was dressed in a pristine white shirt and shorts with a white belt to match attached to which was a revolver. Now my mind was starting to work overtime. I was going to be arrested, taken to a filthy jail with no food and only contaminated water to drink. Fortunately the policeman could speak English so I immediately explained to him that I had been taking a photograph of two ships on the horizon (which I had seen earlier) and that the ladies had thought I was trying to take their photo. I said to him most politely that I apologised if I had offended them in anyway.

It was my lucky day, for the policeman, in perfect English, politely told me that he understood and directed me to go, while he would sort out the irate ladies. I eventually caught up with Dennis and Bob further along the beach and after telling them of my little escapade, made it clear that I had not been happy about them running off and leaving me on my own. They thought it quite amusing and said they had their own problems for after running half the length of the beach when they stopped there was the bracelet seller waiting for them. We never got rid of him till we arrived back at the hotel!

That evening we were invited to a meal with the some high official known to our agent and our director. We were picked up by car from our hotel and driven through what appeared (as it was dark) to be most of the back alley type roads of Lagos. Bob, Dennis and I were not too happy about the route we were taking and the excessive speed we were travelling on such narrow roads, or should I say dirt tracks, we felt we were being kidnapped.

It was when we eventually turned into a dimly lit back yard that I was sure we had been kidnapped, for there in front of us standing in the glare of the car headlights, were four huge black Nigerians standing in a line with white aprons wrapped around their middle. It's strange how in a situation like this you always suspect the worst. I whispered to Bob and Dennis before getting out of the car, that I thought we were going to be butchered by the reception party!

The yard we were in was in the form of a huge square. At one end was a covered section made out of corrugated iron sheet under which was a long trestle-wood table with wooden forms down each side and a chair at one end. At the opposite side were two coal burning braziers with a small table each side on which were laid raw chickens and the largest snails I have ever seen, they must have been at least three inches in diameter.

The yard was illuminated by two naked electric light bulbs one over the table and the other above the braziers. Surveying this scene reminded us that we were invited out for a meal and that we were not going to be butchered, thank goodness! Introductions were made to our host whose very large physical appearance conveyed that he obviously enjoyed his food. We sat down at the bare table and were given a paper napkin each and a pint of the local beer. By this time I was really hungry for I had not eaten anything for about eight hours. Anyway, whatever we were going to eat smelt good.

The first course was, as you may well have guessed, roasted snails. They had been removed from their shells once cooked. Each of us had six of these snails to devour. Our host speedily tucked in signalling that we should follow suit. Our director did not need any persuading for he had been to one of these meals before. I gingerly took one of the snails between thumb and forefinger (there was no cutlery) and took a bite. I can only describe it as trying to eat a piece of Dunlop's best car tyre. I turned to Bob who was sitting next to me and to my amazement there he was tucking into these snails with gusto. On realising that I was still chewing my first piece of snail, he reminded me that it would be an insult to our host if we did not show that we were enjoying the fare before us. Our host, seeing that I was struggling to get through my second piece of rubber, courteously suggested I leave the rest. By this time I had downed several pints trying to get the snails down, so I was feeling very warm and pleasant, even though I was starving of hunger and wishing we had dined in the hotel where the food was reasonably good.

The next course was peppered chicken which came in three grades, 'mild', 'hot' and 'hang on to your hat'! I chose the mild one which proved to be delicious. I was ready for a second one and like my host tucked into it with gusto as I was still pretty hungry. It only took one bite for me to sense that the whole of the inside of my mouth felt it was on fire. I had been given one of the hottest peppered chickens, much to the delight of the rest of the party assembled. What made it worse, I had to wait for someone to come and refill my empty glass before I could quench this burning sensation.

That was the end of our meal, a very big disappointment to me for my mouth was still on fire when we left later to go to the airport for our flight home. One of the cooks brought me four snails, still in their shells to take home. I politely accepted them but quickly got rid of them by giving them to our chauffeur. So much for Nigerian hospitality, never again!

After all our efforts, we never ever got a contract out of the Nigerians, not that I was surprised.

45. All Change

BACK IN THE OFFICE I found the work interesting and with a good staff of six estimators, two of whom concentrated purely on Ministry of Defence enquiries and contracts, life at work was enjoyable. Being responsible for electrical estimating and contracts brought me into contact with many subcontractor representatives, for I had the task of negotiating and selecting the successful subcontractor for each piece of electrical equipment. These negotiations covered a considerable amount of money therefore the aim was to negotiate a low price but retaining good quality. The distasteful part of the work was having to push subcontractors to the limit in reducing their prices by sometimes telling them white lies. It was a cut–throat business which had to be done to stay competitive with other shipyards competing for whatever contracts were being quoted for.

On the bright side, there was the basic designing of the electrical systems and the compiling of the specification for such systems which I enjoyed, even though we were working to very tight deadlines. Then there was the benefit of the Christmas presents from the various company representatives. These presents varied from diaries, bottles of spirits or wine, pen sets, ties and food hampers. There was one particular subcontractor director who I did quite a large amount of business with, on hearing I was going to change my car suggested that I leave everything in his hands. No way was I getting into that dangerous league of bribery. Eventually, the company stopped all individual gifts being accepted and decreed all should be put into a pool and raffled for the benefit of the whole staff.

After a number of years heading the electrical estimating department, the company decided to have a complete departmental reorganisation. The electrical department was totally reorganised. I was moved into the engineering design department which was housed in a separate building at the top of the bank away from the main offices. This building housed not only the engineering design but also the naval architects department and on the floor above, the estimating department. This meant that I now came under the control of the engineering general manager who answered to the local engineering director. My title now was electrical engineering design manager.

My work continued to be the same except that after a few months I was relieved of the electrical estimating section which moved into the estimating department so that I could concentrate on designs and specifications for both merchant and naval vessels. This meant the design work for an estimate could be produced in a more detailed form for the estimators by my department and if the company was successful in gaining a contract then a detailed design and specification was developed and produced for the drawing office. Although I was a bit apprehensive at first, I really enjoyed working in this department.

The general manager was a chap called Bob Gowdy who I got on well with and whom I respected. Bob did have a tendency to rush things a little instead of thinking things through first before going ahead. Having said that, he did get the job done and on time. Bob was a devout practising Christian and this was portrayed in his attitude and caring nature towards his staff.

Our director, Bob Wilson was a fairly big man of Scottish descent, from Ayr on the West Coast of Scotland. He was a very competent engineer with an excellent memory which enabled him to be extremely well versed in Shakespeare and he used passages of the great bard to sometimes emphasise his point of view on a topic. He was also prone to the use of bad language when annoyed.

There were two other managers apart from myself, Wal Temple in charge of engineering design and Albert Tonkin in charge of controls. Both these managers were competent in their fields of work and were friendly colleagues. About a year later a weapons manager was appointed called Tim Holt, ex navy personnel. Wal Temple was a gentleman in every sense of the word and always ready to help anyone. If ever you visited his office there was always a warm greeting and the offer of a cup of tea and a chocolate digestive biscuit which were Wal's favourite.

Wal stuttered now and then but it never prevented him from expressing himself at meetings where his profound knowledge of engineering was always appreciated. He also liked a joke and invariably when I visited him he would be keen to relate his latest one knowing full well that I enjoyed telling and listening to jokes. We would often walk down the bank to the manager's restaurant telling each other our latest funny story.

One lunch break we set off down the bank and he started to tell me a joke. Between stutters, I invariably used to try and help him get his words out, not always the correct ones mind. He had managed to tell me half the story when we almost reached the restaurant. He was really finding it hard to say a particular word this day and I had not guessed what it was. By this time he was really frustrated but then just as we were about to enter the restaurant he turned to me in a calm voice and said "Bugger. I'll tell you it, tomorrow!" Well that to me was even better than the joke he told me the next day. That was Wal, full of fun and ready to joke about his difficulty in getting certain words out.

It was a sad day when Wal retired as he was liked by everyone. Retirement did not prevent him from visiting the office occasionally, for he liked to keep up to date with what was going on in the shipyard. Every time he visited the office he always provided the managers with a chocolate Penguin biscuit each and a tin of biscuits for the designers to share. A lovely, kind and thoughtful man who I shall never forget.

After about a year we all got a shock when we found out that the office had to get rid of a manager. It was unfortunate that Albert was the one selected to be made redundant. Our director informed me that I was to be responsible for taking over the controls section as well as continuing as electrical manager. It was not a happy situation taking over someone else's job, who I had known and respected for many years but I had no other option.

Controls was not a favourite of mine but with an excellent staff to support me I became more competent. Bill Knox became the new engineering design manager when Wal retired. A good choice, for Bill had been Wal's section leader for many years. Bill was also a nice guy, very knowledgeable in his field and a good friend. Bill's favourite expression whenever you met him was "Hello Bonny Lad". He and I had a very close working relationship through the design work we were involved in.

Tim Holt was a typical navy man who tried to impose some of his naval practices into the office without a great deal of enthusiasm from the rest of the designers. He did try hard and finally persuaded the staff to clear their desks before leaving at the end of the working day for the sake of security, which he himself strictly imposed.

Having settled into the design department I found the work most interesting and enjoyable, particularly for the fact that I had a very competent team of designers. As I said before I was always at my best when the pressure was on. My nature was and still is to be neat and tidy, hence my office was the same with my desk cleared each evening before leaving.

Being involved with design meant I had a very close working relationship with the naval architects department and particularly with the Chief Naval Architect, Dennis Brown, the life and soul of any party. Dennis, like me, enjoyed a joke and a bit of fun. He was good at sketching and renowned for his home-made cartoons of various characters within the office, particularly of yours truly. Dennis and I travelled together on numerous occasions, representing the company at meetings both home and abroad and on each trip there would be some prank, amusing incident or remark instigated by Dennis.

46. Back to Singapore

Dennis, bill knox and i were sent out to Singapore on one occasion to assess the work involved in modifying a cargo vessel which was lying in the dry dock at the local shipyard. The following day after our arrival we went down to the dry dock to inspect the vessel. After a hard morning's session of climbing around the ship in a temperature well into the high eighties, Dennis said he needed to go down into the bottom of the dry dock to inspect the outside hull. As Bill and I had completed what we wanted to see, we accompanied him. Although we each wore a boiler suit and an old pair of shoes, we were not prepared for the conditions at the base of the dry dock. It had not been cleaned out after the hull had been sprayed with high pressure hoses hence all the mud and sea slime was lying six inches deep. Trying to walk through it was like being on a skating rink. We completed the inspection after about twenty minutes by which time the mud and slime was now seeping into our shoes which made walking even more precarious. We managed to stay upright on our feet until Dennis placed one foot on the bottom step of the concrete stairs leading to the exit of the dock and slipped and fell backwards into the mud and slime. I went to help him up but in trying to get him on his feet by gripping his hand in mine I went face down. What a mess we were in, it was a good job we had boiler suits on. We eventually managed to get to our feet by raising ourselves on all fours, much to the amusement of Bill.

There were no washing facilities so we just had to remove our boiler suits and hire a taxi to take us back to the hotel. The look of surprise on the receptionist's face when we walked into the hotel was a picture when she saw the state of Dennis and me. Thinking back I'm sure I didn't slip when I grasped Dennis's hand, I'm sure he purposely pulled me down - just the sort of prank he would pull.

After a quick shower and a snack lunch we all met in the hotel garden where we relaxed and cooled off in the swimming pool. Yes, we all agreed that we deserved the afternoon off after the hot and sticky morning we had experienced. Yes, this was the life, relaxing by the pool and enjoying all of the comforts of our five star hotel.

After about an hour, completely relaxed and starting to cool off with a nice pint of the local beer, who should walk in on us but the Managing and Contracts Directors, Alex Marsh and Ken Chapman, who unknown to us, were staying at the same hotel. "This is what we pay you for", was the opening remark of Ken smiling. Bill and I were too gobsmacked to reply and left Dennis to relate on our morning's escapades. After updating them both on the proposed modifications to meet the ship requirements, I think we convinced them that we had not been skiving.

As we could not get a flight back to the UK for another three days, the rest of the time was ours. Just one of the perks of the job! Most days, Alex and Ken were in negotiations with a ship owner trying to clinch an order, while Dennis, Bill and I passed some of our time away by looking around the city of Singapore and doing some shopping, for this was the place to get bargains.

I remember buying two pairs of leather dress shoes for a total of fourteen pounds. I also bought a length of patterned material for Joan to make a dress. How did I buy the right amount? I explained to the assistant which material I wanted, said it was for a dress to fit a slim five foot four and a half inch lady with a modest bust size. No problem for the assistant and Joan was delighted with my choice of colour and pattern.

Ken Chapman knew Singapore like the back of his hand, for he had lived there for many years in the past and was based there to negotiate prospective contracts with owners in the far-east region. Alex and Ken really looked after us the few days we were there. Each evening they would take us out to a different place to eat, either an upmarket restaurant or outside at some little Chinese stall that Ken would recommend, both an experience in their own right and strictly no snails!

One late afternoon we all went down to the shopping mall to buy presents. I happened to mention that I could do with a haircut. Ken said "I know just the place. When you go in, ask for a head massage after the haircut - it's refreshing". I decided to follow his suggestion. Seated in the chair, the others left and said they would call back in an hour which I thought was a long time for a haircut. The young, beautiful, dark haired Singaporean lady, in a dress split at both sides up almost to her waist, took only ten minutes to cut my hair. Then after washing and drying it she started massaging my scalp with her fingers and letting her nails brush through my hair. I have never experienced such a soothing and yet tingling and calming sensation as I did then, it was so peaceful and relaxing that I almost fell asleep. It was not until I was aware of four faces peering through the window laughing at me that I reluctantly decided it was time to leave much to the disappointment of my masseur who wanted me to stay for further treatment. When I met up with my colleagues and asked what was so funny, Ken asked me if the lady had invited me for more treatment. On confirming she had, he said "I guessed that, your next massage would have been in private with nothing on". I was not for the full massage but I really did enjoy the head massage.

Singapore at the beginning of December was a sight to see in the evening when all the Christmas lights were switched on. It was quite unique in the fact that all the main shopping streets and malls were lit up by thousands of tiny clear lamps, similar to what we would normally have on our Christmas trees. The whole effect was a mass of twinkling stars. The shops and hotels were all lit up with the same type of lamps only these were coloured with each establishment creating its own individual design as there was a city prize for the best display. The whole city was a sight to behold, I have never seen any Christmas illuminations so artistically and colourfully displayed.

Our last day in Singapore was a Sunday and as our Directors had no business that day, Ken decided that we should have a walk down to the famous Raffles Hotel. On the way there my watch came off my wrist and broke on the pavement. "Not to worry" said Ken. "We will get you a new one on the way to the hotel." After a good half hour walking we came upon some street traders selling watches and jewellery. Ken contacted one of the traders who he had obviously dealt with before and told him to give me a good deal on a new watch. I was offered a brand new stainless steel automatic Rolex copy watch with gold figuring, magnified date recording, for twenty five pounds. The copy watch is identical to a real Rolex to look at except that the movement is a different make. After a little bartering I bought the watch for fifteen pounds, a real bargain, for it had a very good make of movement within the case and it lasted me for about fifteen years. It was only because the winder broke that I had to stop wearing it because no watch repairer or jeweller would touch it with it being a copy watch and hence illegal, otherwise I would still be wearing it today.

To be sitting in the lounge and savouring the ambience of Raffles Hotel where Noel Coward and many others of equal fame had sat was a unique experience. There was the smart uniformed young boy parading round the lounge with his paging board which everyone read to see if it was them being paged. Even though it was only eleven o' clock in the morning, Ken insisted we each sample the Raffles famous gin sling for no-one visits Raffles without having this drink. Quite an interesting and pleasant morning was had by all and we all left with a glowing feeling inside, nothing to do with the drink of course!

Dennis, Bill and I left Singapore at about nine on Sunday evening on a long journey none of us were looking forward to, as it was around eighteen hours flying time. Fortunately we were travelling Business Class so after our meal, it was heads down for most of the journey.

47. Norway

ONE OF THE PLEASURES OF WORK is when you and your staff have contributed to getting a successful contract. Negotiations for one contract began by sending a team of four out to Oslo in Norway. The team comprised Bill Gardner (Contracts Local Director), Bill Wilson (Engineering Local Director), Jimmy Grey (Estimating and Contracts Manager), and myself (Electrical and Controls Manager). The visit was in December, just before Christmas.

We landed on a snow covered landing strip in Oslo Airport in the late afternoon. My first taste of Norway was speeding along at seventy miles per hour along a frozen snow covered road in a taxi with the driver in complete control of his vehicle heading towards the capital. It felt a bit scary travelling at that speed on such an icy road but later I was assured by the driver that the car had special winter tyres fitted which prevented the car from skidding.

The whole country is well prepared for the severe winter weather. Even the tram lines were steam heated at the junction of each set of rail points. You could not help but admire the resourcefulness of the Norwegians in dealing with the severe weather conditions. Of course, we the English visitors had arrived fully prepared in sheepskin or heavy top coats and gloves. Or so we thought; for none of us had thought about bringing, boots or wellingtons. The crazy thing about it was none of us attempted to buy the right footwear while we were there, we all just ruined our shoes in the snow.

The first day we ventured outside the temperature was minus eighteen degrees centigrade, the coldest temperature I have ever experienced. When you breathed in, you could feel the cold air passing down into your lungs.

We changed our hotel after the first couple of days for we were not happy with the food, particularly the dinner at night. While the meat and fish were good, there were no vegetables. This was not really to our standard for a five star hotel. We eventually moved into a small family hotel which was much more to our liking. That is all except Bob Wilson who continually moaned about something every meal. It got to the stage where the rest of us would have to get in quickly and say how much we were enjoying the food before Bob could comment, otherwise he put you off the meal altogether.

Breakfast was unusual to say the least, for our fellow Norwegian diners would have fresh cold herrings, sardines or some local fish delicacy, together with jam, marmalade or honey spread on bread and all eaten together. An unusual combination as far as we were concerned.

Each day we visited the Norwegian shipping company Leogh Hoeg for discussions on the separate sections of the proposed ship's specification. Then in the evening we would either dine in the hotel or visit a restaurant and then perhaps go to the cinema to see a film which usually had English sub–titles.

I found Oslo one of the cleanest cities I've ever visited. No graffiti, chewing gum, or waste lying around. The Norwegian people were very friendly, very much like the Geordies with their sense of humour. I learnt my one and only Norwegian phrase after the first day and that was only because people passing on the street would call out "God Yule", which means "Merry Christmas". I did pick up other words from our meetings with the owners and that was because they sounded very much like some of the Geordie expressions.

Being Christmas time, everywhere was decorated as in any capital city, the only difference being that in most shop doorways there would be a candle burning. This feature puzzled me for days until I found out that it was an ancient Norwegian custom, a sign of welcome, which I thought was a nice touch, being Christmas.

As my Engineering Director, Bob Wilson, and I were the first to complete our proposed specification discussions with the owners, we had a spare day to ourselves before returning to the UK. We both agreed to visit the Olympic ski jumping bowl at Holmen Koln, way up one of the mountains.

We boarded a train which would take us to our destination. There were about five or six station pick up points for skiers going to the top of the mountain. Bob and I must have looked out of place amongst the rest of the passengers who were all dressed for skiing. Bob dressed in his heavy navy blue top-coat, scarf, gloves and ordinary dress shoes. I was similarly dressed except that I wore a brown sheepskin coat.

Somehow or other we missed Holmen Koln station where we should have alighted and finished up at the top of the mountain which was the terminal station where all the skiers got off. Once everyone had alighted the train moved off away from the route we had come. There was no station, just a wooden platform. There was no information either about the trains so we did not know when or where the next train was coming or going from.

Off went the skiers across the flat topped mountain giving Bob and me a curious look, wondering what two typical English gentlemen were doing at the top of a snow covered mountain without skis! Bob and I stood there watching the skiers until they were out of sight then we suddenly realised that here we were, all alone on top of a mountain standing in freezing snow with no means of communication with anyone and no idea if there was going to be another train.

Across from the platform was a snow covered track where the snow had been pushed to each side to a height of about four foot, leading down the mountain side. We decided that we ought to try and get down by foot as we did not fancy being stranded up there all night. We set off, reached the track which we could now see twisting and turning as it descended down the mountain at a fairly steep gradient.

I marched off first onto the hard packed snow, followed closely by Bob. Then it all happened, I suddenly started to slide down the track slowly getting faster and faster and performing uncontrolled pirouettes until my feet went from under me and I landed up at the side of the four foot wall of snow. On looking around I saw the funniest of figures sliding down the track with arms waving, shouting in his brusque Scottish twang, "how do I stop?" Yes it was Bob. I did not have time to tell him for he went into the wall of snow backside foremost. I was in stitches with laughing although I dared not let Bob see me doing so. When he eventually picked himself up, a snow covered, saturated form said to me in the choicest of foul language I have experienced, "who's ----- -- idea was it to come up the ------ mountain?" I had to turn away for I could not stop laughing as his knee length top coat had crept up his back and there was his shirt tail hanging out of his trousers, soaking wet. When he discovered this there was another burst of foul language which could only be interpreted by another Scotsman. Incidentally I had not escaped untouched for with wearing a short sheep skin coat, my trousers got soaked and of course both of us had snow inside our shoes. We hung on together and sheepishly tried to make our way down again but to no avail for Bob suddenly let go of my arm and went sliding diagonally across the track into the wall of snow on the opposite side. Amid fits of laughter, I managed to stay upright by staying close to the wall of snow. As we were just about to set off once more there was a Norwegian family slowly ascending the track from side to side on their skis. As they passed, Bob politely asked them if there was a hotel further down the mountain for we had seen some form of building in the distance. Fortunately like all good Norwegians the father could speak a little English. He said to Bob "which hotel?" Bob in his frustration and totally forgetting his manners, replied "any ------- hotel".

I'm not sure the Norwegian understood what Bob had said but he did indicate that there was a hotel further down. It must have taken us about two hours to get from the top of the mountain down to the hotel. We ended up in a very large room which was just like a log cabin where meals and drinks were being served. On one side of the room was a large log fire burning which Bob immediately made a bee line for so he could dry his shirt-tail. It was a good job there were few people in the room to witness Bob standing in front of the fire holding his shirt tail out behind him in an effort to dry it. After a bowl of hot soup and a hot drink we both felt a lot better. We discovered on leaving the hotel that we were at Holmen Koln, our original intended destination. The famous ski jump had to be seen to be believed. I had seen it on TV, when the camera looked down the ski slope but it didn't compare to seeing the actual slope which looks almost vertical from top to bottom. I was very impressed and thought to myself how brave Eddie the Eagle, the one and only British ski jumper must have been to attempt such a jump.

It was fortunate for Bob and I that we had come down from the top of the mountain as there were no more trains going up that day, all other trains terminated at Holmen Koln. I suppose once they had taken the skiers up there was no need to go up again for there would be no passengers to bring down, except for two lost English gentlemen!

48. Satisfaction Before Wealth

O<small>N COMPLETION OF</small> the specification negotiations, our team returned home with hopes high that we had satisfied the wners requirements. We were invited by the owners to return to Oslo a few weeks later where we concluded negotiations and finally landed the contract to build a very sophisticated cargo ship named 'Hoegh Duke'.

It is hard to explain the feeling in helping to secure an order. For apart from the exciting culmination of creating the design and compiling the specification, there is the knowledge that there is a lengthy period of future work for the draughtsmen and tradesmen who have to develop and build the vessel as well as keeping the company in profit.

Over the years spent in the Design Office, I had the privilege of representing the company individually or as part of a team at home and abroad on many occasions.

Life was good at this time, I was enjoying being involved in design work, I had a good team of designers and I enjoyed the companionship of my fellow managers and director. I was also happily married to Joan with two beautiful daughters, my own house and car and an active social life. What more could a man wish for?

Many colleagues were seeking jobs with sub-contractors who paid very high salaries. The money was substantially higher than that paid at Swan Hunters but they sacrificed their family life by having to work away from home and invariably abroad. No way was I tempted, I had a good job which I loved and found interesting and above all it was fairly secure work. Too many ex-colleagues returned to Tyneside to be with their families only to find that there was no work for them and certainly not at the salaries they had been used to. Some said that it was best to get away and gain experience in different fields of the profession. They may be right but as far as I was concerned the position I was in did not warrant giving up the security and happy family life that I enjoyed.

Trips abroad were always a nice change from being stuck in the office, not that I minded that but it was interesting visiting different countries. Mind you, there was always work to be done. It was not the 'jolly' that Joan used to imply just before I was setting off on a company visit abroad! It was on one trip that I learnt a very important lesson.

There were about seven managers being sent out to Baltimore in America. It was my first flight in a jumbo jet. I could not believe the size of the interior of the plane. We were travelling Business Class as usual and departed at about four thirty in the afternoon. We had no sooner sat down when the stewardess placed a large glass of champagne in front of us. This was consumed quickly before being replaced with another. By the time we had settled down and consumed our drinks it was time to order an aperitif before dinner was served. I was now beginning to feel a warm glow inside and was talking excessively. With two small bottles of wine consumed with the meal followed by a large port it was time to go and empty the sewage tank! I don't remember how I got to the toilet but on leaving I remember seeing a whole row of empty seats which I made a beeline for and on which I stretched out and fell asleep for most of the journey. I felt much better after the sleep but that experience taught me never to over-indulge when there's free liquor on offer and to this day I never have any alcoholic drink when flying.

On our arrival at Baltimore we were taken to the Merchant Navy Officers Club where we were to stay for the next five nights. This club was opulence itself, better than any five star hotel I had previously stayed in.

Our purpose for being there was to examine an old passenger liner that had been laid up for about ten years to see if it could be extended and refitted for service. On our first visit to the ship we got quite a shock. It was like a ghost ship - everywhere was covered in dust and cobwebs and to make matters worse there was asbestos fitted throughout the whole of the vessel. This meant we all had to wear protective clothing. Well, if you could have seen us all, each one of us had a toughened white paper boiler suit with hood attached, protective plastic over-shoes, a pair of cotton gloves, a set of goggles and a protective mask to cover our nose and mouth. We looked like a team from outer space and, of course, my boiler suit did not fit properly which meant the boiler suit legs were at half mast and the end of the arms just came past my elbows.

Then there was little Bob Gowdy, totally lost in his gear which was far too big for him. The scene was hilarious to say the least. We went around the ship in pairs in case there was an accident as there was no lighting on board, and all we had was a torch each to find our way around. It was weird at times for you would be walking along the passageway and suddenly two ghostly forms would appear with their torches directed underneath their chin illuminating only their goggles and mask and each uttering some hideous moan to try and scare the other - acting just like kids again!

Being a large vessel, each pair could be walking around for hours without seeing anyone. This meant it was deathly quiet and eerie at times. We found a cabin which had obviously had someone sleeping in it as there were signs of food and yet we were told no one was living on board, it was all very strange. I remember walking through one of the passenger lounges and seeing all the tables and chairs laid out with coffee cups and ashtrays just left where they had been placed ten years ago except they were now covered in dust and cobwebs, most weird.

When the team met up that night in the Officers Club, we all agreed that apart from the cold and damp conditions, there was a strange, ghostly atmosphere on board.

After a couple of days working in the damp and dusty atmosphere, we had a free day where the Club provided us with a limousine and chauffeur to take us around the capital, Washington. We viewed all the tourist sites including the

White House and Capitol Hill. We then drove back through the downtown area where you dared not stop for there were black gangs on most street corners ready to relieve you of your possessions. Not a pleasant experience, we were all glad when we were back out on the open road, although our driver, also a black gentleman, took it all in his stride. What a lovely person our guide was and how knowledgeable about his country, he made every place we visited so interesting, nothing was a trouble to him and his humorous remarks and deep bellowing laugh kept us all amused on the journey.

On our last working day on the ship I was paired with my boss, Bob Gowdy. Our job was to examine the engine room, a place where you had to be extremely careful moving around for certain walkway plates, unknown to us, had been removed. One minute I was following Bob along a narrow walkway chatting away to him when suddenly there was a thud, his light went out and all went quiet. Unfortunately my torch battery was spent and there I was standing in the pitch dark, not a sound to be heard. I shouted to Bob to stop fooling around and switch his torch back on as it was dangerous. I waited for what seemed like an eternity before a voice shouted from the depths of the engine room bottom, "I'm here, I've fallen through a manhole and I've dropped the torch". By this time I dared not move in case I befell a similar fate, however after a lot of moaning and groaning, a light appeared - he had found the torch. I suggested he stay put until I could get some assistance or at least a new torch. We eventually got Bob out and he appeared none the worse for his experience although he was not happy that my colleagues and I found it amusing. That night before going in for dinner we all met in the bar lounge for a drink. The conversation got round to Bob's disappearing act in the engine room and this set me off relaying how I had been talking to myself at one point when Bob had gone down the manhole. This escapade had everyone laughing and with the help of the drink, it appeared funnier than it really was. It was not until we started laughing that Bob, who had seen the funny side of the event himself was in agony, shouting "Don't make me laugh, I think I've bruised my ribs". Well, by this time most of us were crying with laughter, totally ignoring poor Bob's agony. The next day Bob saw the doctor who diagnosed that he had bruised his side but had done no serious damage, though he would feel sore for a number of days. I have never been able to fathom out why it is so amusing to see or hear about someone else's mishap.

We left Baltimore the next day. We did not get an order as the company decided against going ahead with the extension and refurbishment and as far as I know the ship might still be lying in Baltimore harbour rotting away to this day. In one respect it was a blessing we did not get the order for there was a tremendous amount of asbestos on board which, if not handled right, could be a killer.

I suppose one could say that this trip had been 'a jolly', certainly a jolly good laugh!

49. Flights

Travelling by air has never been a problem for me although there have been some flights which have strained the nerves a little. The first was when a group of us left Newcastle Airport to fly to Heathrow on our way to Norway. We took off in a thunder storm, never got above cloud level and for the whole fifty minute journey the aircraft vibrated and bounced up and down. Then on approach to landing due to strong winds the plane nose slewed to starboard which convinced my colleague and me that we were not going to make the runway. The plane did eventually straighten up but landed with a severe bump onto the runway. Not a pleasant flight to say the least.

The second was in an eight-seater light aircraft hired by the company to fly us down to Bath for a presentation meeting. It was on the return flight that I was invited to sit next to the pilot. What a fascinating experience, particularly as it was at night. The explanation by the pilot of the flight details and seeing the various cities and towns on our flight path made my day. Approaching Newcastle Airport we were met by strong winds which, like the previously described flight, tended to slew the aircraft to one side as it was small and light. It was quite hair-raising to watch the runway coming to meet you from the cockpit with the plane vibrating and slewing so much. Fortunately the pilot warned me that as soon as he had lined the plane up with the runway he would be putting her down hard to stop the wind lifting her back up. We were almost onto the runway before the pilot got the plane under control and brought her down successfully with a bump. Another nervous flight but one not to be missed.

50. Cruising

My FINAL TRIP ABROAD for the company was to fly out to America with three colleagues, namely the Shipbuilding Manager, the Joinery Manager and the Hull Estimating Manager. The purpose of the trip was to examine a cruise ship owned by the Carnival Cruise Line with a view to extending the vessel amidships. The ship was on scheduled cruising in the Caribbean and Bahamas from its home base in Miami.

We flew out from Heathrow and arrived in Miami where we checked into a very nice hotel close to the harbour. The following morning instead of eating in the hotel restaurant, we decided to try one of the famous American diners. We were not disappointed, ham and eggs (sunny-side up of course), hash browns, sausage, beans, tomato, mushrooms and fried bread, followed by waffles smothered in maple syrup, all washed down with as much free coffee as you could drink. What a way to start the day!

We boarded the Carnival Cruise Line vessel 'Festival' just after lunch at Fort Lauderdale, where nearly all the cruise liners terminate their Bahamas and Caribbean cruises. It really is a sight to behold with ten or more liners lined alongside the various quays, and I wondered where all the passengers came from to sail on all these cruises.

Our party was allocated two twin berth cabins in the passenger accommodation which proved to be very comfortable. Meals were taken in the Engineers' Mess where the food was mainly served to suit the Italian officers. There were no complaints from us for it was a change to eat Italian food. As

I said before, our purpose in being on board was to assess the design changes required to lengthen part of the accommodation section of the vessel. The ship's manager's job was to assess the overall feasibility of the project, the Joinery and Estimating managers were to consider the accommodation changes and I was to assess the engineering and electrical modifications required.

We could have completed our tasks in two days but unfortunately the next flight back to the UK was another three days away. This was no hardship for us for here we were cruising on a luxury liner, working in the mornings only, with the rest of the day to ourselves. After lunch we would find a comfortable deckchair by the swimming pool on the sun deck, relax and watch the passengers enjoy themselves. This particular cruise was geared to catering for the young American students on vacation, hence there were many bikinis on show. It was on this particular job (dare I call it), that I discovered the obesity of some of the American women. There were lots of them and most were a tremendous size, easily in the region of thirty stone or more, and they always seemed to be eating throughout the day. Some of the younger girls had quite pretty faces but then it was all spoilt by this huge bulk of flesh waddling along beneath it. What a shame that such beauty should go to waste.

One afternoon, my colleagues and I were lying on the deck by the pool enjoying the sunshine when I noticed a few yards away this huge mother and equally huge daughter sitting on deckchairs. They were chatting away in a very customary loud American drawl while at the same time each devouring a large hot dog. That's the beauty of cruising you can eat any time of the day, if you're so inclined.

Getting back to the very large couple I was watching and listening to, I was intrigued by the way they were eating their hot dogs. It was like watching a mechanical shovel: hand to mouth every second without a breath in between! Worse was to come...after demolishing the hot dogs the daughter decided that she needed to cool off in the swimming pool. Incidentally, by this time they both had the attention of my colleagues. The girl walked slowly (she could not do otherwise due to the amount of flesh between her thighs) to the steps of the pool turned and started to descend backwards down the steps holding on to the handrails. Halfway down the steps she became stuck between the handrails. As much as she tried, she could neither go up or down the steps. A distress call to mother brought her waddling to the scene. Several attempts were made to dislodge the daughter but to no avail. Eventually, and to the surprise of everyone around the pool, for they had now attracted everyone's attention with their commotion, the mother placed her bare foot against the daughter's stomach and gave a mighty shove which sent her reeling backwards into the pool.

We were all pleased to see the girl freed from her predicament but we did not appreciate that there would be a huge tidal wave that swamped us all as she hit the water - we were absolutely drenched! I don't want to appear rude to the afflicted but this episode should have been caught on camera. Afflicted is perhaps not the right word as there did not appear to be any control over their eating habits and they only had themselves to blame for getting into such a state.

As guests of the Carnival Cruise Line we were free to use all the ship's facilities and participate in passenger activities. Evenings were spent writing up our reports then either watching a show or having a quiet drink in one of the many lounges on board. One evening, we all went into the casino with the sole intention of watching others gambling their money away on the gaming machines. We were intrigued at the operation of one particular hand operated machine by a very large black lady. As fast as she was feeding the machine with discs it was pouring out into the pay trough five to ten times the amount paid in. It was certainly her lucky night for every disc played was a winner. I thought perhaps she was a plant to entice others onto the machines but then she won on other machines too.

We moved on round to the opposite side of the room to find a black man raking in the winnings off a similar machine just as the lady had done. Seeing how easy it was to win and we were all thinking the same way, Bob, our project manager suggested we all have a try. Each of us purchased ten pounds worth of discs which made a total of forty pounds to gamble with. It took no more than two and a half minutes to lose the lot. I have to say I felt sick inside at wasting so much money in so short a time. I said to my colleagues that I would have had more satisfaction throwing it over the side of the ship than feeding it into those machines. I felt really gutted but then I wasn't a gambling person and never have been. Mind, I might have been recording a different tale had we won!

There were four ports of call during the four days we were on the cruise and by kind permission of the ship's manager, we all got ashore to view this beautiful part of the world. The first was Nassau, capital of the Bahamas. The second was San Juan, the seaport capital of Puerto Rico, part of the Caribbean. The third, a beautiful small island called St. Thomas a few miles east of Puerto Rico and the fourth and final port of call was St. John's in Antigua, part of the Leeward Islands, another beautiful tropical paradise.

It was from St. John's that we disembarked and flew to New York where we just managed to catch the last flight of the day back to the UK. One of the better trips I and my colleagues experienced representing the company. But to no avail, for the Cruise Line decided not to go ahead with the project as I believe it would not have cost much more to build a brand new vessel (which they did in later years). Bad news for the company but good news was to come quickly afterwards.

The Falklands War in 1982 had a major effect on shipbuilding as far as Swan's was concerned. Having lost a number of vessels in that war, the Ministry of Defence decided to replace them. In doing so Swan's gained orders for the building of some of the replacement vessels which, although welcome to the workforce at that time, was tinged with sadness at the memory of those lost in those tragic circumstances created through war.

51. Politics

ONE OF THE PROUD ACHIEVEMENTS for the yard in that year was the completion of the aircraft carrier 'Illustrious' which was handed over to the Ministry of Defence twelve weeks ahead of schedule so that she could join in the battle of the Falklands.

This was a glowing tribute to the tremendous effort put in by the workforce who had responded magnificently to the MOD request to speed up the completion date. Three years later, another of these giant aircraft carriers was completed bearing the proud name of 'Ark Royal', the fifth ship to bear this name since the late fifteen hundreds. She consequently became the flagship of the Royal Navy.

As time progressed the company was relying more on Ministry of Defence orders as we found it difficult to compete with the foreign yards on merchant ship orders. The foreign yards had a much cheaper labour force thereby keeping prices ridiculously low and most contracts were heavily subsidised by their governments. Even the MOD contracts had to be won under fierce competition from other yards in the United Kingdom. Swan's had built up a reputation for providing well designed, quality ships with a workforce second to none. The biggest problem which loomed on the horizon was the fact that there were too few orders for the number of shipyards which meant some of them had to close down. Even though it meant less competition, I always felt sad when a yard had to close for usually some time in the past I would have made acquaintance with one or more of their staff.

The hard part about losing a contract is not about losing it on a lower price or a better design but on a political decision. Time and again, Swan's tendered a good price to meet the design required and failed to achieve the order purely based on political decisions. This certainly opened my eyes to the political wheeling and dealing that went on over major contracts particularly in the reign of the Conservative government of the eighties. I am convinced to this day that their aim was to close down the shipyards and heavy engineering industries. Here we are an island nation surrounded by water and yet we had to rely on the French to build Cunard's new flagship, Queen Mary 2. The Cunard Shipping Co. at one time would never have dreamt of having a liner built anywhere other than in Britain. If it had been a French ship to be built, no way would they have allowed the British to build it even if we had the resources to do it. The Tory government has a lot to answer for as far as the decline of British shipbuilding and engineering industry is concerned during their decade in office and I speak as a Tory at that time.

During this quiet period we were quoting for almost anything that if successful would keep the workforce occupied. From quarter million ton tankers we were now quoting to design and build river ferry boats and other small vessels. The design departments were kept busy investigating designs for the offshore oil industry platforms, oil drilling ships and even the design of wind powered generators long before they came into operation.

52. Redundancies and Retirement

WHEN I FIRST JOINED the company pension scheme in my early twenties, no one at that time thought about pensions until they reached the age of sixty five. It was not until later in my working life that I decided that I would attempt to retire at the earlier age of sixty, having seen and heard of so many colleagues dying either just before retirement or just after. My plan was to enjoy at least five years (if not more) of retirement. Here I was now approaching my sixtieth birthday and with the company struggling to achieve orders.

The situation got so bad that in the June of that year the company announced that voluntary redundancies would be accepted. My colleague Bill Knox and I calculated what benefits would be achieved by retiring earlier than we had intended and it worked out a very favourable proposition. We both applied for voluntary redundancy but only Bill was successful. In one respect it was nice to know that the company wanted my services but on the other hand I was disappointed that I was not leaving the company for the atmosphere throughout was at a low ebb. As a manager, one of the worst two decisions I ever had to make was selecting those for compulsory redundancy and worst of all having to inform them that they were to be made redundant.

Just before the end of the year the company once again announced that there would be redundancies issued providing volunteers were not forthcoming. As I was planning to retire in the following February, I decided to apply but first I made sure with my director that I would be accepted. I informed him that after having given forty five years service to shipbuilding, I felt that I warranted taking advantage of voluntary redundancy. My conversation with him was successful for when the voluntary redundancy list was circulated my name was included. Just before the company Christmas break of 1992, a farewell retirement presentation of a wall clock (my choice), was given to me by the head of department in front of staff and close colleagues from throughout the company. This was followed by a further farewell event at the local hostelry.

Little did I realise that within four months of my leaving, the company would pass into receivership. The yard was not finished yet, for in June 1995 a new company was formed, Swan Hunter (Tyneside) Ltd. headed by a Dutchman named Jaap Kroese who, through his perseverance and business skills, managed to keep the yard open. This was encouraging news to those not in employment and indeed to those of us who had retired.

A few months prior to retirement, the general engineering manager and I were assigned to assist a small private ship design team situated further down the river Tyne. They had acquired a contract for designing a lighthouse and buoys maintenance vessel which was to be built in Lithgow's shipyard on the river Clyde. As there was no one with engineering and electrical design skills in their team, we at Swan's assisted them. This meant many trips by the Engineering General Manager and me to the owner's office in Edinburgh and visits to Lithgow's shipyard who were to build the vessel. As the contract with Swan's was still ongoing after I retired they invited me to continue working for the design team but as a private consultant. This meant that I continued to work for two or three days a week after retirement for about two months up to the ship's sea trials which I was invited to attend.

I was offered further design work on contracts mainly situated in Scotland which would have been quite lucrative but I was ready for retirement. Having said that, I found the first few months hard to settle down at home for I missed the company of my colleagues and the technical conversations within the Design Office. I found it difficult just to switch off from all the technical jargon of design work after so many years.

Nevertheless, once I got organised into a settled routine with more time to devote to my hobbies and new interests, and of course spending more time with Joan, I finally settled down to enjoy a very happy retirement.

53. Conclusions

Having been fortunate to cruise on P&O and other company liners since retirement and sampled life as a passenger, I find I still get an exciting tingling feeling whenever I'm aboard a ship.

Shipbuilding and the Merchant Navy gave me the opportunity to visit twenty two different countries throughout the world. I look back now over forty five years of involvement with ships and realise how fortunate I have been throughout my career and how grateful I am to so many. First for the guidance and encouragement offered by those experienced personnel in the early years of my career. Secondly, for the numerous opportunities presented to me by directors and managers of the companies I worked for. Thirdly, for the help and companionship of all my working colleagues. And last but not least, for the patience and understanding of Joan during my many trips abroad and late evenings at the office.

Given the chance to change my working life, I can honestly say that I would not alter it in any way. The love of ships and shipbuilding has and always will remain in my life.

I trust that it will continue for many more years to come.

Lightning Source UK Ltd.
Milton Keynes UK
UKHW020639180722
406010UK00010B/1372